Falling in Love Again

Falling in Love Again

The Mature Woman's Guide to
Finding Romantic Fulfillment

Monica Morris, PhD

SQU P ERS

Cover Designer: Phaedra Mastrocola
In-House Editor: Joanne Abrams
Typesetter: Gary A. Rosenberg

Square One Publishers
115 Herricks Road
Garden City Park, NY 11040
(516) 535-2010 • (877) 900-BOOK
www.squareonepublishers.com

Library of Congress Cataloging-in-Publication Data

Morris, Monica B.
  Falling in love again : the mature woman's guide to finding romantic
fulfillment / Monica Morris.
    p. cm.
  Includes bibliographical references and index.
  ISBN 0-7570-0136-X (pbk.)
1. Man-woman relationships. 2. Older women. 3. Dating (Social customs)
4. Love. I. Title.

HQ801.M779 2005
306.73—dc22

2004018832

Printed in the United States of America

10   9   8   7   6   5   4   3   2   1

Contents

Acknowledgments

To my publisher, Rudy Shur, heartfelt thanks for your encouragement, your advice, and your enthusiasm for this book from the very first day we spoke of it.

Thank you, too, to my editor, Gene Friedman, whose suggestions and insights were invaluable, and to Elaine Kennedy, for her never failing good cheer and common sense.

In addition, I would like to thank Veronica Shoffstall for allowing us to use her beautiful poem *After a While* (© 1971 by Veronica Shoffstall) found on page 148.

I also want to express my appreciation to the hundreds of men and women who so generously shared their stories with me and from whom I learned so much, and to colleagues, friends, and family for their continued support and interest in this project.

Finally, this book is dedicated to Clark. He knows why.

Preface

Wanting and needing love in our lives is perfectly natural at any age. It isn't something to be ashamed of or to deny. It doesn't mean that we are needy or dependent or weak. It simply means that we are human. Human beings thrive on love. Admitting that we want love is the first step to finding it. If you've picked up this book, then its title speaks to you; it's meant for you. Keep reading—and if you allow yourself to follow just a few of the suggestions and ideas you find here, if you arm yourself with just some of the tools, then at the very least your life will be enriched. It may be transformed!

Who am I to suggest how you might look for love? As a sociologist, I've spent many years teaching and writing about social relationships. Far more important, though, has been my experience as a widow, a woman who perhaps was just like you, looking to fall in love again. The tools presented in this book were shaped directly by my adventures—and the adventures of hundreds of single men and women in their fifties, sixties, and later, whom I interviewed and who were generous in sharing their stories. I learned a lot—but then, I had a lot to learn.

My mother certainly never taught me much about men. Her experience was limited to just one man, my father. She was sixteen when she met him. Her most compelling lesson, and I learned it well, was that I was to be a "good girl" because no decent man would want "damaged goods." Following my mother's lead, I married an endearing young fellow I met when I was eighteen.

Having already been fed up with pretending an interest in combustion engines and silly sports—and with struggling to hang onto my virtue—I gladly hung up my dating-game hat. We planned to live happily ever after, until death did us part, and we did. Then, after forty good years, I was on my own for the first time in my life—and doing what I never expected to do again: dating.

It was so strange to be single in a city like Los Angeles. It is a unique metropolis with threads of nuttiness woven into its fabric and diverse communities scattered across a hundred miles. My dear friends, adult children, and caring colleagues all helped ease that terrible transition from wife to widow. Finally, though, I was on my own, too busy to be lonely, but aching for the taken-for-granted sharing of everyday events, the ordinary routines, and the talking. Most of all, I missed the talking.

Nevertheless, the idea of meeting someone didn't enter my head. From the life-cycle courses I had been teaching, I knew that for every widower over fifty, there are at least five widows. Over and over again I'd heard that old cliché about all the good men being either married or gay. I'd had a fine, long-lasting partnership with a sweet and loving man. That part of my life was over. Or so I thought.

Some months into my widowhood, a colleague who had passed me in the halls for over a decade with no more than a nod and a "Good morning" invited me to lunch. In turn, I boldly asked him to a concert a couple of weeks later. He turned up at my house wearing a long-out-of-fashion dark suit, trying to dress appropriately. This being Los Angeles, appropriate dress for the symphony can be anything from a tuxedo to cut-off jeans! Still, his effort was touching and appreciated, as was being driven to the concert hall and delivered safely home.

Once home, what was I supposed to do when he followed me up the steps and into the house? I had no idea. Fortunately, my colleague was a gentleman, and his interest in me was probably more compassionate than passionate. Whatever his motives, his concern for me helped at that difficult time. To have an attentive friend, yes, a man, call for me, take me out, and bring me home—a date, yet not really a date—was wonderfully life affirming. It helped me move from the state of being "much married" to that of being a *single woman* rather than a widow, a title I had already accepted as mine for the rest of my life.

My colleague was to be the first of dozens and dozens of dates. Given the statistics, how could that be? Widowers are scarce and women outnumber men at every age after high school and college. I discovered, however, that the recent trend to later-life divorce brings a large addition of single men seeking female companionship to the pool and, often, to marriage. If I, a sociologist, hadn't known this, surely other women needed to hear the good news, too. So I decided to write this book.

For the purposes of "science," I found myself doing things I might never have done otherwise. In a little over a year, I met more than a hundred men, one or two vile and disgusting ones, but most of them pleasant and personable. I've made more good friends than I can count, and I have even been honored with some serious marriage proposals. (I'll save the story about the one I accepted for later on!)

I wanted to learn the best ways to find and meet potential partners for people long out of school or college, perhaps even retired from the workplace. I also wanted to discover what the current expectations were between couples. I was happily married when men and women became "sexually liberated," so the concept had no significance for me at that time. Now, it was terrifying! How was I, rather shy outside the lecture hall and decidedly naive in these matters, to meet men? How was I, who had been one of a couple all my adult life, to venture out as a single? What was the first step?

Throughout that first step, and all the steps that followed, I learned the hard way, by trial and error. I discovered firsthand, as well as from hundreds of mature men and women, what works and what doesn't when setting out to meet members of the opposite sex. What you will find in the following pages is the result of all that: a straightforward, nuts-and-bolts guide to looking for love in a changed and changing world. The tools you will find here, the do's and don'ts, the gentle encouragement, will help you develop the confident attitude you'll need to venture into the previously unknown. The resources provided here—where the men are and how to meet them, as well as ways to enrich your life and make the most of each day—have been tried, tested, and rated. I wish I'd had this book in my hand when I started out!

Wearing my researcher's hat was a neat trick! It gave me license to explore the new and mysterious world of relationships far more daringly than I might otherwise have done. It was almost all enjoyable! And even what was not fun was often funny—at least in hindsight. Along the way, I also learned that I could still fall in—and out of—love. Finally, I'm not quite as naive about sex as I once was. My mother might not want to know that. You, though, reading this book, should have no doubts. Read on!

Falling in Love Again

1

It's Not Too Late to Fall in Love

I'm willing to bet that you never thought of yourself as a pioneer. But you are! You and I are walking where many have not walked before. The wonderful news is that we are living longer and are in better health than any people in the history of the world. We should be celebrating that, but along with the improvements that bring us ten, twenty, thirty extra years of life have come some changes in the way we live—changes we didn't bargain for. Not so long ago, a woman in her fifties or sixties who had lost her husband—and she was usually widowed rather than divorced—was thought of as an old lady whose life was nearly over. That was the way she saw herself, too. She stayed home, knitted sweaters for her grandchildren, and took care of others for the remainder of her life.

In today's world, if you are in your fifties and beyond, you are no longer "old." You have years and years ahead of you. Unfortunately, there aren't any instruction manuals that show you how to spend that time. The challenge is to take those added years, that gift, and fill them with life and love—as well as with knitting, if that's what you enjoy. It's a challenge because you know you have to make it happen, but you aren't sure where to begin. You may be shy about venturing out, afraid of what you might find. You may feel a bit foolish admitting, even to yourself, that you would like to be "fulfilling" yourself in some way, or that you might enjoy the company of a nice man. It may have been a long time since you were single—and you are unsure of yourself.

Well, take heart! Help is right here. In these pages, you'll find encouragement to cheer you on. You'll find tools to help you develop the self-confidence and courage you need to be a pioneer. "Life shrinks or expands in proportion to one's courage," wrote Anaïs Nin. So, be brave! The confidence to be brave comes with:

- having reasonable expectations
- understanding the situation
- understanding yourself
- knowing you have done the best with what you have
- knowing you are prepared
- getting involved in the world
- having something to say for yourself
- knowing that what you want is "normal"
- knowing you can look after yourself

And that is what this book is all about. It is designed to help you gain the confidence and knowledge you need to get the most enjoyment and fulfillment out of your life.

WHAT ARE YOUR EXPECTATIONS?

At a "conversation group" recently, one of the questions put to me was: "If you could choose among all the film stars or entertainers in the world, who would you pick as your 'type'? What kind of man turns you on?" After a few seconds of thought, I realized that I don't favor any particular "type," and that my fantasies about a mate have little to do with a man's face or form.

The group persisted. "But what would the man of your dreams look like? Not only his appearance; what qualities would you want?" They wanted me to give them some "ideal"—and an "ideal" is not, and never can be, real. To satisfy the others, I managed to list a few necessary characteristics. He would have a good sense of humor, be intelligent and kind, be in reasonably good physical shape, have a political outlook similar to mine, be able to make good conversation, care about music . . .

One problem for people at any age is this concept of the "ideal" partner who will look like a film star, meet all our intellectual needs, satisfy our passions—and take out the garbage as well! That perfect person is out there, somewhere, and we will recognize him at first glance. Electricity will crackle between us. Our eyes will meet and we will both know that we have found the perfect mate.

If only it were so!

Chemistry Is Not the Same as Love

Chances are that the very strong connection you might feel at first meeting with a member of the opposite sex will last only for a short while. You may be drawn together by an overwhelming and irresistible desire that quickly pulls you into each other's arms—perhaps into bed. You won't be able to keep your hands off each other. Sound familiar? It happened to you when you were in high school. It could, and often does, happen between people in their mature years, too. The "chemistry" between the two of you can be so compelling that those "desirable characteristics" you listed for your ideal mate fly out the window. So what if his politics are to the right of Attila the Hun and you are a socialist? So what if his idea of a fun evening is listening to big band music, and you are crazy about country western? You are temporarily insane!

At best, and it happens for some people, the fire will cool down a little, and with time, you will be able to judge each other's suitability more sensibly. You will learn that you do have a lot in common, find that you like each other, and build a firm foundation to a lasting partnership. Just as likely, or perhaps far more likely, the flames will soon consume themselves and you will wonder what you ever saw in each other. He's rude to waiters, he's vain beyond belief, he's never on time, he's frugal to the point of meanness . . . and so on.

The myth of love, or fierce attraction, at first sight sometimes causes a turning away from someone who might, in time, prove a suitable match. A well-known matchmaker told me that she had negotiated successful marriages between people who *hated* each other at first sight and wanted never to see each other again. Based on her examination of their tastes, likes and dislikes, spiritual beliefs, and dearly held values, she knew they were well suited, even if they didn't know it themselves. She insisted that the couple persist in getting to know each other; she wouldn't allow them to give up too soon.

Examine Your Attitudes

If you're looking for romance—whether you are widowed, are divorced, or have never been married—it helps to be realistic about what you will find. Some would-be suitors have told me that widows tend to fall into a number of categories. Some canonize their lost husbands, erasing their flaws from memory and recalling only their better, sweeter, or more generous ways. Their minds hold this polished and perfect creature as the standard by which to judge any new man who might come into their lives. It's a hard act for any man to follow.

On the other hand, if a woman divorced after many years of service to her husband and family—and especially if her husband left her for another, often younger woman—her sense of loss and grief is real and painful. These feelings may be expressed as bitterness and suspicion. Often, these women perceive men as being "users and takers."

If you envision "the men out there" as never being able to measure up to what has been lost, or as being unfaithful by nature, you are surely handicapping yourself in the search for a man with whom to share your life.

Women are also pretty hard on *themselves* and see themselves negatively compared with the way men perceive themselves. A classroom exercise used in training sessions for professionals shows how easygoing men are about their appearance compared with women. Class members are given a set of statements, the object being to find someone in the group—and the age range may be from twenty-five to sixty-five—to answer "true" to each of the statements, including "I feel good about my body." An instructor for the course told me that, in the many times he has carried out the exercise, he has hardly ever come across a woman who agrees that she feels good about her body. Women have all kinds of reservations about themselves even if they are working out and lifting weights, and look perfect to everyone else.

To find people with a glowing self-image, the instructor almost always has to turn to the men in the class. They'll almost always admit to feeling good about their bodies. A man tends to see himself as youthful, virile, and sexy, just as he was years ago—even if no one else sees him that way.

Comics in newspapers reflect what is going on in society. It's the sudden burst of recognition in the image that makes us smile. In a newspaper cartoon by Gail Machlis headed "Blind Date," a man and a woman are talking on the telephone. She asks: "So, how will I know you?" He answers: "Well, I'm tall, about six foot two, and I used to have red hair." Another by Wise and Aldrich captioned "Personals," shows a newspaper column with an advertisement reading: "SM (single male)—slightly balding, wears glasses, but only for reading, enjoys lawn mowing, walks to get the paper, napping, just sitting around. Interested? Write Box 402."

Let's face it. Most of us, men and women, are pretty ordinary. Mr. Ideal, by definition, doesn't exist. That doesn't mean you should accept just anyone, but if you are to be successful in finding a romantic companion, you should have realistic expectations of him and have a candid—not negative—picture of yourself.

In my early ventures into the dating scene, I quickly learned of the inflated descriptions men give of themselves in personal ads, in letters, and on the telephone. Besides overstating their looks, especially their height, they often understate their age. I was amused that one man advertised himself as a "young widower, fifty-eight," thinking you'd have to be ninety to consider fifty-eight as young. (I believe it was Collette, the French author of *Gigi*, who yearned, "Oh to be fifty-five again!") After our first pleasant meeting, "young widower, fifty-eight" confessed he was, in fact, sixty-one—and had been a widower for more than ten years.

"Why would you fib about so *few* years?" I asked.

"I think sixty is the dividing line," he told me. "To say 'sixty' in an advertisement is the kiss of death. No one will respond."

That was his belief, but it is far from true. Men who advertise their age as over sixty, or even over seventy, receive many responses, as do women who request a companion of "sixty plus" or "sixty to seventy" or "sixty-five to seventy-five." Even if a woman doesn't include her own age, the implication, at least, is that she too is in these age groups.

Don't Let the Statistics Frighten You

It is well known that single women over fifty, whether they are widows, divorcees, or never married, outnumber single men of that age. Women, in fact, outnumber men in all age groups after the college years, and the gap increases with age. Statistics, however, can be misleading. If a woman takes them too seriously, they can—and will—stop her from even trying to find a partner in her later years because she feels her chances are small to none.

It helps to know how to interpret the figures. For example, there are statistics that lump all the over-fifties together with people in their eighties and nineties, and even those over one hundred years old! On average, women are still more likely to live longer than men, although it is encouraging to note that the age gap in longevity is narrowing. When the figures for very old women are averaged in with figures for those in their fifties and sixties, the odds can be ten to one or even higher, especially in some residential areas.

The fact is, far more single women than single men are found in retirement communities like the "Leisure Worlds" and "Sun Cities." In a singles club in one such community, the women are referred to as the "Casserole Brigade." These women use their cooking skills to woo new widowers! In spite of the occasional matches that are made in retirement communities, if a woman really wants to find a new partner, she might perhaps consider living in a less age-segregated place.

If we waited for "new widowers," the odds would be truly formidable. As I've noted, women are far more likely to outlive their husbands than husbands are to outlive their wives. Some women outlive two or three husbands! There are now five widows to every widower in the United States, and widowers have higher death rates than married men in the same age groups. But in this modern world, there are some modern trends, and one is the later-in-life divorce. Most of the "fifty-plus" single men are divorced, not widowers. Of the some one hundred men I have met and "dated" in researching this book, only three or four were widowers and only two had never been married. Both of these never-married men had had "long-term relationships" that ended either in the death of the woman or in a divorce-like parting.

The trend to later-life divorce brings a new pool of men—and women, too—into the dating scene. Newly divorced men may relish their "freedom," and some are decidedly "giddy" at first, but after a year or two, many begin to feel the need for a steady or permanent relationship with a woman close to their own age.

In their book *Our Turn*, Christopher L. Hayes, Deborah Anderson, and Melinda Blau discuss research into later-life divorce which indicates that many women do *not* want remarriage. In one study, close to half of the sample of 352 divorced women age forty to seventy-five, all of whom had been in marriages lasting from ten to forty-eight years, did not wish to remarry. Although they missed someone to share their lives with, they loved being independent. While it may not be possible to generalize from this study, it does indicate that not all women included in those "five or ten women to one man" statistics are or will be looking for remarriage.

Get Involved in the World!

Consider this. Even if we were on a level playing field and the numbers of older single men and women were equal, they would never meet each other if they stayed home and watched television. Meeting members of the opposite sex means being actively involved in the world rather than passively waiting. Perhaps your friends will introduce you to someone nice. It does happen—but don't hold your breath!

Good men won't fall into your lap, any more than good jobs will when you need employment. You have to be out there hunting. And you won't expand your mind without making some real effort to participate in an activity that stirs your imagination. One way to do that is to join groups and organizations and take classes that sound like fun—and not *only* because you might "meet someone," though that certainly can and does happen. One of my woman friends, divorced when she was fifty-six, took up square dancing in an effort to get in shape and have fun doing it. She married a fellow do-si-do-er within twelve months. Another friend, divorced at fifty-seven after a marriage of thirty-seven years, wedded a man she met overseas during a two-year stint with the Peace Corps.

It's wonderful if it happens, but as everyone will keep telling you until you are sick of hearing it, you should be opening yourself up to new experiences so you can continue to grow intellectually and artistically. Still, it doesn't hurt if you have lively and interesting stuff to talk about when you do meet a man you'd like to know better.

Get out and do things! That's easier to say than to do, as I well know. When years of social events have been shared with a partner, it is devilishly difficult to venture out on your own, especially if you are shy or feel unprepared, ungainly, and unglamorous. In the beginning, it takes courage and spirit. And you won't necessarily enjoy everything you try.

I'll never forget my first temple dance for "fifty-plus" singles. I still smart at the unpleasant memories of dances I went to in my teens, the agony of standing at the edge of the dance floor *longing* for someone to ask me for a quickstep or a fox trot. So why would I inflict this on myself again? For research, that's why. It was just like being sixteen again except now I prayed that I *wouldn't* be asked to dance. The men all seemed like my grandpa. Most had foreign accents, just like my grandpa, and all were fifteen to twenty years my senior—although they *were* energetic dancers.

I did dance, however, much more than I had in my teens! The band was good, and being whirled around the floor to the jitterbug tunes of the 1940s was quite exhilarating. Few men of "fifty-plus" were here; most were seventy-plus or even eighty-plus. The women were generally a lot younger.

At this point, ballroom dancing wasn't really my cup of tea and I left the dance hours before it was over. Still, I *had* taken my first step into the new and unknown singles world. I had gone out on my own, I had spoken to strangers, I had been invited onto the floor—and I learned I was free to leave if I wanted to! You don't have to do anything you don't want to do, but do be open to experiences outside your own four walls!

PREPARE YOURSELF FOR YOUR NEW LIFE

You've decided that you'd rather not spend the rest of your life without the company of someone of the opposite sex, whether just for the occasional date or for the long term. You are willing to get out into the world and have some new experiences to see what you can find.

Are you ready? Or were you so comfortable in your marriage that you feel you let yourself go? Do you think that no man would find you desirable, that all the other women "out there" are younger, better looking, more self-assured, thinner, and so on? So how are you going to prepare yourself?

Think back to when you began dating as a youngster. For many of us, those memories have faded, but try to bring them to mind. Remember the kinds of preparations you made to go to a movie or for a soda with someone you thought cute or handsome or just nice? At that time, you were experimenting with your looks—using face packs, steaming your pores open and closing them up again, trying on different colognes and perfumes. As a girl, you spent hours styling your hair and putting on your makeup before a date, and you endlessly applied creams and lotions for acne and other skin blemishes. You also tried on all the clothes in your closet. You agonized over which was the most flattering thing to wear, which color would best bring out your eyes (and his!), which dress would hide your baby fat or make more of your nonexistent bosom—and draw attention away from that new pimple on your chin!

And in the flash of an eye, or so it now seems, you were married, had reared a family, had seen the children out of the house, and had lost a husband. And in all that time, only rarely did you spend as much time preparing for an outing as you had when you were single.

Couples who have been together for a long time hardly even notice what their spouses look like. This can be maddening when a husband doesn't comment on a new dress his wife is wearing. But this taking-for-granted attitude in a long-lasting marriage is less a sign of familiarity breeding contempt than of the pair having so much in common, having grown together in such a way, that each sees the essence of the other rather than the surface, the decoration.

Of course, we do pay some attention to our appearance, especially if we work in front of the public. Some of us have our hair styled regularly, and we try to keep our fingernails neat and polished. But in a secure partnership, the intense interest we used to have in every pore of our skin and every hair on our head is replaced with other, more pressing matters.

Well, here you are, single again—in some ways, feeling adolescent again, experiencing the same doubts and insecurities about your attractiveness and desirability that you felt in your teens. And you may find yourself once again taking hours to prepare for a date. Men, of course, are also concerned about the kind of impression they make when they are meeting someone. I can't tell you how touched I was when I happened to see this nice man of about seventy, who has since become one of my dearest friends and confidants, carefully combing his hair as he came up the steps to my front door to fetch me for our first real date—just like a teenager taking out a new girlfriend.

In present-day America, far too much emphasis is placed on youthful beauty as the ideal for which we must all strive. Those of us whose teens, twenties, thirties, and forties were long ago, are still prodded to push back the years by advertisers, the media, and, increasingly, cosmetic and laser surgeons. Women, and men too, spend millions of dollars each year in efforts, usually futile, to look ten or fifteen years younger than they really are, and to weigh fifteen pounds less than they really should. We strive for baby-soft skin that only babies can have, and we try to wipe away all the natural signs of aging, including the lovely laugh lines that give testimony to a lifetime of smiling.

This is not a battle cry to let ourselves fall apart! Most of us are going to live long lives. Medical researchers now estimate that if a woman has reached sixty without any major medical conditions, she will probably live another thirty years. So it is essential that we take care of ourselves, do some exercise, eat plenty of fruits and vegetables, be as attractive as is realistic—and plan to enrich those added years for ourselves and for those around us.

No one would deny that looks are important when meeting new people, but be comforted in knowing that men and women are drawn to each other for all kinds of reasons. Among the people I interviewed was Emily, a widow of seventy-one. Her husband had died two years before I met her, after an illness lasting nearly a decade. In his final years, he was confined to a wheelchair, unable to walk or to do anything for himself. He spent most of his days sitting in front of the television, feeling deeply depressed.

Emily, too, suffered from all kinds of ill health. She had severe arthritis, and had had a hip and two knees surgically replaced not long before our meeting. I walked slowly by her side as she limped painfully to a restaurant near her house. Hardly anyone would have seen her as attractive in any conventional way. Nevertheless, she then had, and still has, an attentive, active, loving man in her life. She met him at a political rally, a fundraiser for a congressional candidate. He adores her and would like to marry her. She says "No way!" For the time being, at least, she is savoring her release from the responsibility of physically caring for another, and is enjoying the courtship and companionship of her "wonderfully tender lover."

You Don't Have to Be a "Ten"

You may think you have to look like Susan Sarandon or Catherine Deneuve if you are to enjoy the friendship and love of a member of the opposite sex. It is worth noting that dazzling celebrities do not necessarily look so dazzling before the makeup artists have done their work. Once, while on a promotional tour for a book, I was interviewed twice by a talk-show hostess, first for her national television broadcast and then, a few days later, for her radio show. I hardly recognized her on the second occasion. On television, her skin had looked like flawless porcelain, her hair was a masterpiece of design; she was drop-dead gorgeous! She arrived for the radio broadcast in what appeared to be her husband's old raincoat, wearing scarcely a dab of blusher or lipstick, and with her hair scraped back into a rubber band. No one would have given her a second look. I'm willing to wager that the "beautiful people" aren't much more beautiful at home than the rest of us are!

In my experience, and in that of the men and women I have interviewed, grown-up people look more for compatible company than for glamour—although, let's face it, glamour has its points! As you venture into or reenter the dating world, you will be more successful if, besides being concerned with appearance, you have something captivating to talk about, are doing something in the world, and can speak about what you are doing in an entertaining or lively way. And, of course, it will also help if you pay attention to the other person's stories!

BECOME AN INTERESTING PERSON— AND A PERSON OF INTERESTS

The most boring men and women I met in the course of collecting material for this book were either retired, and did nothing all day but watch television; or were still working, but did nothing in the evening but watch television. Why would any man want to spend his time with a woman like that, even though he might understand her situation and might have even walked that path himself?

It isn't easy to get back into life after losing a husband to death or divorce. Cooking, cleaning, remembering to change the bed linen, getting up to go to the office or store, even gassing up the car, seems to require more energy than you can find. "What's the point of it?" you might ask, even if those chores give some shape to the day. The very thought of going alone to the movies or the theater or out for a meal may make you shudder. Better to stay home. Good friends and caring sons and daughters are a blessing at this time, but they have their own lives to live and other commitments; you know you can't depend on their compassion forever.

It's important to keep in mind that things can get worse before they get better. We all have our own stories to tell. For me, it unfolded this way. I went back to the university only a week or so after Manning, my husband, died. My days were filled, as always, with preparing and presenting lectures, talking to students in my office, meeting with colleagues, and all the other familiar routines. Domestic responsibilities doubled because Manning and I had always shared the chores, and now I had more to do than hours to do it in. My busy life left me little time for thinking about myself, for mourning, or for loneliness.

Then, after about a year and a half, the university offered an early retirement package so attractive it would have been foolish to refuse. I was eligible by a fluke and, knowing my job might disappear at any time and that I could lose all the benefits of this special retirement offer, I accepted. Fine! I was walking on air—for about five minutes. Then I began to grieve. I mourned for my job, and I grieved for Manning as I had not allowed myself to grieve before. All I could see before me was an enormous void. Everything I loved and that gave meaning to my life was gone.

Ultimately, we have to find a new sense of meaning and fulfillment, discover new pleasures, and find new happiness. We've been told over and over that healing takes time, but until we are healed, we aren't ready for new companionship; we aren't in the right frame of mind.

Almost against my will, I gradually pushed myself back into the world of work, service, and satisfaction. I found that I was qualified to teach homebound, handicapped children. This was a new kind of teaching for me. At the same time, I began volunteering at the local chapter of the American Red Cross. There, besides finding ways to use my research and writing skills, I was encouraged to become a contract teacher for the organization, and was soon so involved with all these activities that I had no time to think about "poor me"—at least during the day.

Before very long, I found that I couldn't do so many things at once; I had to choose. Working with handicapped children can be very satisfying; a teacher who takes on just one child at a time sees remarkable progress. But I found it a little isolating compared with the "workplace teaching" I was doing for the Red Cross. Although not many people would believe it, I'm really rather shy, and talking to a room full of people is one of the few ways I can express my otherwise hidden, "hammy" side. It's such a high to get a crowd of people to laugh!

Eventually, I did "workplace" teaching a couple of days a week, and also gave one day a week to International Services, a program of the American Red Cross that traces people who have been separated from their families by war or civil unrest. I also took the various courses offered by the Red Cross for its instructors and the community. I continued to learn, to meet dozens of people every week, to feel I was doing something useful—and to build a reservoir of fascinating stories, both funny and dramatic, for the entertainment of my friends and family.

You will find your own new interests, perhaps building on your work experience, as I did, or perhaps exploring work or leisure activities that are completely different from anything you've done before. A lot will depend on whether you need to work part-time or full-time, or you have enough income from pensions and other assets to retire from the paid work force. Try on different activities for size until you find just what suits you.

Even if you are financially secure, you may feel that you should be paid for your work. Since the early days of women's liberation, a lively debate has centered on the idea that women have for too long given their time and energy without receiving compensation. You will come to your own conclusions about this, based on your own views and circumstances—and on the availability of paid work where you live. Volunteering your time to a cause you believe in can make you feel wonderfully purposeful and generous, which is no small reward when you are weighing costs and benefits. Becoming involved in your community, whether with a charitable agency like the American Red Cross or a free clinic, or with a local orchestra or theater group, will get you out of the house and into a group of like-minded people. You'll be astonished when you see just how many organizations you can choose among, including artistic, political, charitable, religious, and educational. And you will be welcomed and cherished as a volunteer.

Get into something you enjoy, and regard that activity as separate from your search for a new partner. Look at it as mind-broadening and emotionally fulfilling, as giving you an absorbing interest for its own sake, as giving you something to think about and talk about. And of course, there's nothing to stop you from keeping your eyes open, just in case a suitable man happens by!

WHAT YOU WANT IS NORMAL

Should you feel guilty about wanting companionship and affection? Absolutely not. The need to care for someone and, in return, be cared for is perfectly normal. Sometimes, however, your state of mind may not allow you to come to grips with these basic human needs. Your situation—whether you are a widow, are going through a painful divorce, or have never been married—will most definitely shape your attitude. Whether you're feeling unfaithful to a late husband or vulnerable because of a bad relationship, or you simply believe that it's too late in life to find love, these powerful emotions must be understood, addressed, and overcome.

During this process, the people around you may not make it any easier for you to cope with your feelings. There always seems to be someone ready to tell you how you should live your life! About nine months after my husband died, I took off the wedding ring I had worn for forty years and put it in my jewelry box for safe keeping. This was clearly upsetting to an old acquaintance, someone who had known Manning and me for a long time, and had watched our progress from our early days as immigrants in the United States to our raising a happy family together.

"How can you *do* that?" she wanted to know. "People will think you didn't love him!"

I felt like screaming at her, protesting my *undying* love—but managed to control myself while maintaining my dignity.

"You know that isn't true," I said. "But Manning is no longer here. I am no longer a wife; I am a widow—and very much alive!"

While wanting love and affection is normal, to be *desperate* for love, or to *appear* desperate, is to open yourself to disappointment, pity, and, at worst, ridicule. One of Milton Berle's most insensitive jokes concerns the older woman desperate for a mate. A woman is talking to a man who, it turns out, has just been released from prison after many years behind bars.

"What were you in for?" the woman wants to know.

When he answers that he had been serving time for murdering his wife, the woman is silent for a few moments. Then her voice brightens as she says, "Oh! Then you're *single!*"

A woman who had been widowed for a long time told me about some of her experiences as a single person. She had remarried once, and it had been a disaster. Soon after her first husband's death, she was so eager to be a wife again that she entered into an ill-fated marriage. Knowing I was fairly newly single, she was keen to advise me, "If you find a nice man who is interested in you, you shouldn't let him go, not even if he's old enough to be your father. As long as he's a gentleman, what do years matter? *Any* man is better than no man."

This obvious yearning for a man, *any* man, made me feel sad for her. This kind of desperation, this neediness, is likely to turn men away rather than draw them to her. One of my more cynical divorced friends goes to the other extreme. Quoting Gloria Steinem, she jokes, "A woman without a man is like a fish without a bicycle!"

If you are to look for and find pleasant male companionship—perhaps love, perhaps marriage—you'll need an attitude that is neither desperate nor disparaging! Stepping out into the world of single people and using the resources all around you requires realistic expectations and an open mind. It calls for courage and some risk-taking.

LOOK AFTER YOURSELF!

Knowing you can take care of yourself physically, emotionally, and economically is vital if you are to find that needed courage to leave your safe haven and enjoy new experiences. Yes, there are risks to every adventure. In Chapter Six, we'll discuss the kinds of risks you might face and how you can protect yourself against them so you can venture out with confidence and self-assurance.

While being a pioneer takes some daring, it is preparation that is the key to success. So, fasten your seat belt and turn to the next chapter!

2

Like a Good Girl Scout: Be Prepared!

*Y*ou're almost tempted to venture out into the unknown. You *would* venture out, if only what? You were more attractive, sexier, cleverer, taller, shorter, thinner, had better hair? Add any or all adjectives that describe what you see as your shortcomings, including the need to be "younger," and you'll sit at home alone in front of your television set forever. No one's perfect. You really know that, but for some reason, you think you must be perfect to attract a mate or a date. What you *do* need—and I'll come back to this point again and again—is confidence.

Confidence is not smugness, brashness, or assertiveness. It means feeling comfortable about yourself and knowing you can help other people feel comfortable too. Confidence and self-assurance can be developed and strengthened. When someone returns your smile, you feel better about yourself. When someone responds positively to your idea or suggestion, your confidence is reinforced. When your cheerful "Good Morning!" is returned, the day becomes sunnier and you feel more closely knitted into the human race. Being prepared for new challenges in life is the surest way to build your confidence.

WHAT DO YOU WANT?

Are you looking for a life partner, or would you simply like someone to go to the movies with on Saturday nights—and wake up with on Sunday mornings? Would you like a companion for exotic travel, or are you more interested in hiking in the hills near your home with a pleasant member of the opposite sex? Is the company of a good conversationalist what you would most enjoy? Or would you like someone who can play a musical instrument or sing so you can make lovely music together? Would you prefer to be with someone who just wants to enjoy home life, who will appreciate your good cooking, and who will take an interest in the garden? Or . . . ? You may not know exactly what you want until you know who you are. Further, the answer may change with your circumstances, as you may change, as "Janine" and "Frances" changed.

Janine's Story

"Janine" was widowed after a good marriage of thirty-eight years, and she was sure she wanted to remarry and create a partnership similar to the one she had enjoyed for so long. She had mourned her "George" for over a year and missed the simple routines of her old life. Janine is an excellent homemaker. She loves to cook and always took pride in preparing a fine dinner for George every evening—for which George unfailingly thanked and complimented her. She looked after the inside of the house, painting and hanging wallpaper; George managed the garden, the cars, and the outside painting. After George died, Janine continued her own chores and, as she'd been left fairly well off financially, she was able to hire tradespeople to do George's work. She firmly believed the ideal match for her would be a man just like George.

In the second year of her widowhood, Janine was offered a consulting job as an interior decorator—a job that turned into a full-time position. Her home took on different meaning. It became a weekend haven; a place where she could slip into casual clothes and relax—when her brain wasn't still churning over ideas for blending colors, fabrics, and shapes to be incorporated into her designs. She continued to cook occasionally, but found that housework took too much of her time and energy, so she hired a housekeeper.

The thought of returning to full-time homemaking, with house and husband as her reason for being, lost its appeal. She loved her new professional self, making her own money, being consulted and respected by her colleagues and clients. Yes, she wanted a man in her life, but he wouldn't be another George.

When she met "Harry," a colleague of one of her clients, he was serving on the board of directors of a major company. He traveled extensively, and lived in a full-service luxury apartment that required no maintenance efforts on his part. If he owned a screwdriver, he certainly never used it. The couple married and, a year later, Harry retired with as much annual income from investments and stock options as he had previously earned in his job. For the first time in his adult life, he had time on his hands. To Janine's surprise, and his own, Harry became a handyman, fixing shelves, painting, and doing odd jobs around Janine's house, which they now shared. He discovered George's tools, found he enjoyed repairing things and, finally, began working with wood.

Eventually, Harry became a creative cabinetmaker and began designing and building accent pieces for their own home as well as Janine's clients. Long a knowledgeable wine collector, Harry soon developed an interest in cooking. He took a "cordon bleu" course at the university, and occasionally prepared fine dishes for Janine.

Human beings are dynamic creatures, and what they want and need can change as their knowledge of themselves and of their talents changes.

Frances's Story

At fifty-eight, "Frances" was in a different position from Janine's when "John," her husband, died suddenly. Financially, life had always been a struggle for the couple. John had insisted that Frances be an at-home wife and mother for their three sons—and Frances had been happy with that arrangement. She enjoyed being a housewife, and took pride in shopping economically, cooking nourishing meals, sewing her own curtains, making her own clothes, and knitting all the family's sweaters. When the boys left home, Frances volunteered in the local hospital, working with old people.

The couple had next to nothing in savings, and John carried no life insurance except for mortgage coverage. Their fine house was a valuable possession, but the substantial mortgage had always strained their budget. Even though Frances had no monthly mortgage to pay, the taxes, maintenance, and upkeep of the house ate up almost all of her tiny widow's pension. The little nest egg was soon gone, and she would have to go out to work if she were not to lose the family home.

Her last job, more than thirty years before, had been as a secretary. Her skills were rusty; she knew hardly anything about computers or word processing. What's more, she would have to travel into the city if she wanted a decent-paying office position. Her old car was unreliable, and public transportation from her suburb was poor. Fortunately, she found a job near her home as a clerk in the bookstore of a local private trade college. Although she found the job both boring and tiring, it was simply a means to an end. When she was asked how she liked working in the bookstore, she would answer, "I don't want to talk about it; it's boring, boring, boring." To add a little to her wages, she rented her spare room to a woman teacher, and was irritated at "having to tiptoe around a stranger." Except for the joy she found in her two young grandchildren, Frances didn't have much else to comfort her. She missed John and the simple pleasures they had enjoyed together. Frances longed for her old life. Looking back on it, she could see that their life had been filled with riches.

Only a few blocks away, in the same neighborhood, "Stan" was still recovering from the death of his wife a year before. He had devotedly nursed her through a long and terrible illness, and still felt physically and emotionally drained. His house, built at the same time and by the same builder as Frances's house, was neglected, as was his one-man business. Despite the best efforts of his two adult daughters and three grandchildren to cheer him up, Stan remained lonely and low-spirited. He was also short of funds and knew he must soon find a job or start another small business.

When Frances and Stan exchanged glances across the aisle in the local supermarket, they each sensed that they had seen the other before. Of course! Frances and Stan's wife had been members of the same car pool years before. They had taken turns driving their children back and forth to school. In fact, once or twice, Stan had driven Frances's boys when his wife had other commitments.

As they spoke, Frances and Stan retraced their almost parallel pasts together and realized that their children had known each other and had celebrated birthdays and other events together so many years back. It was the beginning of an acquaintanceship that changed from friendship to affection, and then to love. As their relationship was blossoming, Stan was forced to take a job in the city because he had no capital to start his own new business. He insisted that this was only a temporary measure. Frances, still working at the college, became concerned when she learned that the owner of the bookstore was planning to sell his business. He also warned her that a new owner might not have a place for her. When Frances told Stan about her situation, he said, "But wouldn't that be the perfect little business for us?" Stan saw the opportunity and went for it. He sold his house to raise capital, purchased the store, and moved into Frances's home. The two then got married.

Work at the bookstore took on new meaning for Frances. As an owner, she looked forward to each day's challenges. She and Stan gradually expanded the business, buying other college bookstores for greater efficiency and higher profit. The couple worked well and patiently together. Frances, now a capable businesswoman, is no longer bored at work and has no wish to return home as a full-time housewife. Her wants and needs changed with her circumstances.

The stories about Janine and Frances show us that the question "What do you want?" may have to be phrased differently. Perhaps, "What do you want *right now?*" or even, "What do you *think* you want?" would be better. Neither woman started out wanting to change, and neither could have imagined how her life would be transformed. The way each responded to new situations as they arose indicates the wisdom of remaining flexible in one's thinking. You should take one step at a time, looking for and seizing opportunities as they come your way.

WHO ARE YOU?

One of the most important elements of knowing what you want is knowing yourself. "Twenty Questions"—perhaps more properly called "Twenty Answers"—is a popular exercise college instructors often give to their self-assessment classes. Students are asked to give as many answers as possible—preferably twenty or more—to the question "Who are you?"

When I used the same exercise with my students, I asked both "*Who* are you?" and "*What* are you?" to bring out as many answers as possible. Some could think of no more than four or five answers: "I am: female, a student, Catholic, young, unmarried . . ." I termed these "demographic" answers, the kind you would find in census statistics, not having much to do with who the person *really* is. For those who went beyond these demographic responses, their answers were often quite revealing.

Accentuate the Positive!

For the moment, consider yourself one of my students. Class is in session. As an exercise, take a piece of paper, and see how many qualities you can write down that describe who and what you think you are. Besides the "demographics," what other items appear on your list? Music lover? Artist? Cook? Nature lover? Intellectual? Bicyclist? Knitter? Athlete? Couch potato? Hiker? Dancer? Friend? Typist? Engineer? Sailor? Driver? Sister? Aunt? Go on! There's more. And while you're at it, you might include some of the qualities you *could* have if you applied yourself, some of the things you'd *like* to be. Aspiring writer? Would-be poet? Potential computer expert?

When you have finished your list—and you may think of a hundred items that either *do* or *could* describe you—arrange the items in order of their importance to you. Is playing or listening to music such a passion that your pleasure in living would be less without it? What kind of music means most to you? If you love romantic ballads, could you enjoy the company of someone who finds Frank Sinatra or Tony Bennett boring? Could you be with someone who looks down on jazz, even though jazz excites you so much that you can't keep your feet still when Benny Goodman swings? Of course you could—for an evening or two, or perhaps forever. Only you can decide what compromises you would or would not make for that yet unknown person.

The ordering of your list can give you some clues, too, about where you might look for a mate. You are not likely to meet your match at a Green Party gathering if you are a staunch conservative Republican— although one can never be sure of even that. It's always a good idea to keep your options open. Ideally, however, you should attend events that interest and stimulate you.

By carefully reviewing your list, you can gain great insight into what directions you would like to go. Whether it's mapping out the interests you would like to pursue, or the types of people you would like to date, you'll now have a point of reference based on who you are.

Know Your Strengths and Accomplishments

Too many women tend to downplay their achievements and accomplishments, and emphasize their weaknesses to others and even themselves. Some of us were blessed with parents or grandparents who provided us with a wonderful belief that we can do anything we set our minds to. Others, unfortunately, were not. You may have grown up in an environment that created doubts about your self-worth. If you have only occasionally allowed yourself to feel "superior" in any way, *now* is the time to remind yourself of your good qualities. *Now* is the time to focus on these qualities until you recognize yourself for the valuable and desirable person you are.

Let's go back to the classroom for another exercise. Take a piece of paper and a pencil and begin writing down all the good things about yourself. What do you think other people like about you? How might you make someone else's life better and richer? What can you do well? What *could* you do well if you tried? Include everything good about yourself, no matter how trivial it might seem:

- I manage money well.
- I bake a wonderful pie crust.
- I can organize a good party.
- I'm a good listener.
- I have elegant handwriting.
- I can compose a good letter.
- I have a strong fashion sense.
- I have a good sense of humor.

- I am a great cook.
- I have pretty legs.
- I'm a good dancer.
- I can fix a leaky faucet.
- I play a good game of golf.
- I'm good at my job.
- I know a lot about . . .

As you keep going, you'll realize just how much you bring to the table. Are you perfect? No—but who is? Change does not happen unless you want it to happen. If someone praises you, instead of dismissing it with a quick "no," smile and say "thank you." If you are slow to praise others, consider being a bit quicker. Don't be afraid to tell someone she looks good in that outfit, or that you appreciate what she's doing, or that her new hairstyle suits her. Stop keeping those compliments bottled up.

On the other hand, if you tend to be critical of others, perhaps you need to work on remaining silent instead of blurting out that less-than-kind remark. And remember not to waste your time fretting about something you may have said in the past. Think about *now*! Think positive! Take that list of "the best of you" and pin it on the wall and look at it every day!

Change may not come overnight. There may be one or two setbacks. But if you really work at it, you can be the person you want to be. All you have to do is learn to believe in yourself.

ARE YOU EMOTIONALLY READY?

If you are still hurting deeply from the loss of a beloved husband or the end of a love affair, wait a while. Mourning is a real process that takes time. "But I'll always grieve for my husband," I can hear you say. "He was my life. I'll never forget him."

"Miriam," a widow who claimed she was serious about remarrying, asked me, "How do you think a new husband would feel about my keeping a framed picture of 'Mort' [her late spouse] on display? I just couldn't bear not to see his face every day." I suggested, as gently as I could, that when she met the man she cared enough about to marry, she might be ready to put Mort's picture away. If she couldn't, perhaps it was too soon to think about a new commitment.

A good marriage of long duration can't simply be forgotten, nor can or should the memory of a wonderful partner be put aside. Those shared years of joys and struggles, of rearing children, of successes and disappointments, are part of you, part of what you have become. No new partner who cares about you would expect you to abandon the past or to forget the person who was the center of your life. But he is entitled to be central to your new and future life together. If this expectation makes you feel disloyal, you are probably not yet ready for a new marriage or partnership.

Joanna's Story

"Joanna," widowed just over a year, was ardently courted by "Alvin," a man with whom she felt she had a great deal in common. Alvin's political and religious beliefs matched hers. He was a writer as well as a jazz critic, although he didn't play an instrument. Joanna's late husband, "Daniel," had also known a lot about music and had played in his own band as a semi-professional musician.

Alvin invited Joanna to a jazz festival out of town. This was to be their first time away together, the first time Joanna had shared a bedroom with any man other than Daniel. She regarded it as something of a test. Alvin was head-over-heels in love with her and wanted to marry her as soon as she would name the day. Joanna certainly liked Alvin. She enjoyed his company and his loving attention, but she wasn't sure about the depth of her feelings for him.

After a drive of several hours, the couple arrived at their destination, a small picturesque coastal town. They checked into their hotel and went straight out to the first musical event of the festival, a big band bash. "The audience sat at round tables and listened to dance music, swing rather than jazz, number after number, hour after hour. Dance music is for *dancing*, in my opinion, but everyone there just sat. I found myself getting more and more frustrated, longing to get up and move to the music. Alvin was having a great time, sitting there snapping his fingers and nodding his head, tapping his feet and shouting 'Yeah, Man!' like a silly teenager. When the band began playing some of the romantic songs of the fifties, I found tears welling up and I had to leave the hall to sob by myself in the ladies' room! Those were songs that Daniel had sung to me during all our years together. The Sinatra numbers, especially, upset me.

When I got back to the table, Alvin was still snapping his fingers and nodding and looking really foolish to me. Undignified! I hated myself for being such a pain, such a . . . snob, I suppose, such an ingrate, but I told him I'd like to leave the concert. Would he drive me to our hotel, just a short distance away, and go back and listen to the music on his own? I didn't want to spoil his pleasure, but I couldn't bear to stay a moment longer."

Alvin was very patient and understanding. He did as Joanna asked and returned to their hotel room after midnight, when the concert was over. Joanna heard him come in, but pretended to be asleep. She clung to the very edge of the king-sized bed, curled up tightly, her back to Alvin, effectively shutting him out. He, in turn, kept to the other edge of the bed, hardly moving all night and hastily moving his arm or leg back if it inadvertently touched her.

Joanna recognized that she hadn't finished grieving and that it would be unfair to Alvin, or any other man, to get married again just yet. To use Daniel as a yardstick against which to measure another man was also unfair, especially as her memories of him were selective. "Didn't *Daniel* ever embarrass you—or himself?" I asked her. She thought about the question for some moments before admitting that, yes, he'd had his faults. "He was a human being with human flaws . . ." She searched her purse for a tissue and dabbed at her tears. "But I *knew* them and accepted them . . ."

Traditionally, one year is the time allotted for mourning a deceased spouse, but different people grieve differently. Some people push their grief aside, press on with their lives as though nothing has changed— and then are hit with the full realization of their loss two, three, or even five years later. The world of work doesn't allow much time—two or three weeks at most—for a person to "recover" from the death of a partner and get back on the job. We put on a brave face for the sake of the people around us, shoving our pain to the backs of our minds. But it doesn't go away.

Widows seem to "know" when they are ready to move on and consider looking for a new love in their lives, just as they seem to know when they aren't ready. A dear friend, widowed for three years, had ventured out on a singles' hike for the first time. "It's taken a while, but I know now that 'Doug' [her husband of forty years] would have wanted me to live as full a life as possible. For me, that includes male company. Doug knew I used to be such a flirt, but that part of me seemed to die when Doug died. The flirt is coming back, I can feel it!"

Other widows have told me that while the memories of times shared with their husbands will always remain with them, they finally can recall those times without sadness. They feel ready to begin creating memories with someone new.

While a deceased husband can become angelic in memory, divorce often leaves a residue of bitterness and sadness. Newly divorced people and those recovering from a recently ended love affair are wise to wait until their pain has eased before they look for another partner.

Sally's Story

Having been divorced for nearly twenty years, "Sally" told me of her grief at the breakup of her longtime relationship with "Peter" some three years before. She had mourned him so deeply that she couldn't, wouldn't consider someone new in her life—until now.

"When my *marriage* finished, I walked away and hardly looked back. The divorce was a long time in the making and, if anything, it was a relief to both of us to have it over. The early days of our marriage had been wonderful, but as the years went by, our anger kept growing. We tried counseling, we both tried to change, but nothing worked.

"After eight years of living with Peter, though, I went into such a terrible depression, I wanted to die. He was the one I should have married, but he said he wasn't the marrying kind—even though we had bought a house together and fixed it up. We were married in every way except legally. Then he simply walked out on me. I was in such a bad way, I was put on Prozac for a while! Me, a health nut who never puts anything chemical in my system if I can help it!"

When Peter walked out of her life, Sally's pain was as severe as if he had died. With time—and some professional help—her wounds healed and she knew she was ready to let go of the past and move on.

FEAR OF TAKING THE NEXT STEP

When you feel you are emotionally ready to consider finding love again, you may still be afraid of new situations—of saying the wrong thing and embarrassing yourself. If you find yourself getting tongue-tied or looking away from a person you've just met, perhaps you suffer from shyness. For some people, this feeling is temporary. It disappears after a few awkward moments. For others, the shyness is acute, and can prevent them from meeting new people.

Shyness is surprisingly common. Even people constantly in the public eye struggle with it. Stage fright is a problem for many well-known actors and performers. For example, it is said that early in her career, Barbra Streisand suffered from such terrible stage fright that she became physically ill before each concert, and that the late great Sir Laurence Olivier, too, threw up before going on stage.

People never believe me when I confess that I am shy. For years as a university professor, I stood in front of classrooms filled with people, lectured, often joked, and appeared confident and self-assured. I have also presented dozens of scholarly papers at professional conferences, appeared on television programs, and narrated radio documentaries. The trick for me was to hide the shyness, and that can be done in several different ways.

Know What You Are Talking About

The appearance of self-assurance in professional settings comes when a speaker is completely in command of her material. That takes work. Every fact must be checked and rechecked beforehand, all references have to be in hand, and alternate theories or points of view must be understood so that they can be addressed—and dismissed, if necessary. Effective speaking involves knowing the audience, knowing the subject matter, and being ready to defend your position when questioned. It also involves learning the best speaking techniques, getting rid of nervous quirks or tics, and finally, lots and lots of practice, sometimes with a tape recorder or even a video camera.

I'll never forget the time I caught the professor I most admired—and feared—psyching himself up just before he entered the lecture hall. Usually, I was seated in class before he arrived, but this time I found myself following him down the hall, trying not to let him see me. Because I was in such awe of him, I knew I would stammer if he spoke to me.

The professor stopped at the classroom door, straightened his back, and pulled himself up to his full height. Then, to my surprise, he composed his face, putting on a rather stern expression and giving himself a few seconds to "come into character" before turning the door knob. With his demeanor in place, he sailed majestically into the lecture hall, where the students immediately hushed into a respectful silence. It was only then I realized that this famous scientist was human, and that he quite deliberately put on a mask before facing an audience.

Tricks of the Trade

You don't have to be a professor or a public speaker to use some of the "tricks" that work for professionals. You can develop your speaking skills before entering any unfamiliar social situation. Ask yourself:

- What kinds of questions might you ask a stranger?

- How would you ask those questions so that you appear interested rather than just plain nosey?

- What do you want to know about this person?

- What questions would be acceptable to him?

- How would you answer if those questions were asked of you?

- Can you give a gracious answer to a question you think is too personal?

- What subjects can you talk about with confidence?

- What interests you or excites you? Music, politics, cooking, nutrition, movies, or gardening? Try to bring those topics into your conversation.

- Listen to yourself on tape. Do you like what you hear? Can you change what you don't like?

Write down your questions on a sheet of paper. Read them to yourself, and practice them on your friends. The more you practice, the more natural they will sound to you.

If, after all of that, your shyness still presents a problem, other solutions are available. There are professional psychologists who specialize in overcoming this specify type of anxiety. There are local shyness groups that bring people together to help one another. And there are speaker organizations designed to teach you how to talk in front of *anybody*. Think of it this way: It may be a good opportunity to meet an equally shy guy who has the same aim as you.

The important thing is to do something—anything—to take the next step. Then when you find someone in which you have a genuine interest, you will have the tools you need to break the ice.

MATURITY AS AN ASSET

Before you go any further, I'd like to point out the elephant in the room. It's big and it's heavy, and when it stands in front of you, it can block the view of what's ahead. It's called your age. When I became aware that women in their thirties and forties worry that they are too old to meet a mate, too old to be attractive, I realized how common this lack of self-confidence is at almost every stage of life.

In other cultures, maturity reflects wisdom. Age is meant to be respected. In our modern culture, with its emphasis on youth, the message seems pretty clear—age is something to hide. In fact, there seems to be a conspiracy directed at making us feel unsure about ourselves. Ads show adolescent models selling every type of conceivable product; movies and television shows primarily cater to the young; corporations force out their older employees first; and retirement villages constantly promote the idea that we should live in "our own" communities. It's enough to give anybody over fifty a complex, but I don't buy that for one minute. I believe that life can easily begin at fifty and beyond, and as you will see, current research supports that conclusion.

Those of us in our fifties, sixties, seventies, or even eighties are making history. Lydia Bronte, in her extensive study of long life and creativity (*The Longevity Factor: The New Reality of Long Careers and How It Can Lead to Richer Lives*), sees a "second middle age" added to our lives. She found that the years between fifty and seventy-five can be extraordinarily rich and creative.

Bronte writes of a number of distinct patterns of creativity among older people. Some retire from lifelong careers. They then return to work, but make major changes in their primary interests, taking up writing or art or going into business for themselves. The workplace is no longer as stable as it once was, so Bronte suggests using retirement, especially early retirement, as an opportunity to retool for new careers. Other people, who are not required to retire, simply continue working productively well into their eighties and later.

We are an aging society and as the baby-boomers—the largest group of people ever to be born in the same time period—move through adulthood, being old is becoming sexy! Some of the film stars popularly viewed as "heartthrobs" are certainly not in their teens or twenties, nor are they necessarily conventionally beautiful or good-looking. Paul Newman remains handsome even as he approaches eighty! Many other leading actors and actresses—Sean Connery, Cher, Clint Eastwood, and Harrison Ford, to mention but a few—remain box office attractions well into their sixties, seventies, and beyond.

The judges at a recent "Ms. Senior America" pageant in California expressed astonishment at the elegance, poise, and talents of the contestants, whose ages ranged from sixty to seventy-nine. Not only were the women attractive—"Look at her legs!"—they were also active and energetic, experienced and wise, determined to live every day fully, serve their communities in numerous ways, and continue to learn. Some had taken up music; some had begun new careers; some had developed a taste for adventure and travel. One judge said he was impressed by how many of the contestants referred to things they had done in the past five years. They weren't looking back to when they were twenty or thirty. "It's like they've experienced a rebirth."

This "rebirth" is possible for all of us. It does not mean that we *must* be in the workplace, or that we *must* be in "productive" careers, or that we have to be as glamorous as Goldie Hawn. It does not mean we must be musical or literary or artistic. But being reborn *does* mean looking forward to the future and bringing with us wisdom gained from the past. Our experience is a valuable resource that helps us maintain a sense of balance and reality as we try new activities, meet new people, and live every day as an adventure. We can use those extra twenty or thirty years fully and positively, or we can let them go to waste.

FITNESS AND WELL-BEING

The achievers in Bronte's study of creative older people exercised more often than most in their age group. Physical activity appears to benefit both body and mind. For most of us, regular moderate exercise is enough to maintain healthy hearts and a feeling of well-being. For general fitness, a brisk walk for half an hour to an hour, three or four times a week, is considered adequate by many medical practitioners, although people who have been working out all their lives may feel that much more exercise is necessary.

Some of my friends do not feel right unless they spend at least an hour each morning building muscles at the gym, followed by a half hour swim and some brisk jogging in the evening. They suffer guilt if they skip any of this. Ideally, you'll devise an exercise program that feels right for you, and gives you maximum benefits with minimum wear and tear.

Studies show that being physically fit is a powerful force for health. A team led by Steven N. Blair, director of research for the Cooper Institute for Aerobics Research in Dallas, studied 25,341 men and 7,080 women who received physicals at the clinic between 1970 and 1989. The study found that physical fitness is such a powerful force that even smokers with high blood pressure and high cholesterol who are in good aerobic shape, tend to live longer than nonsmoking couch potatoes who are otherwise healthy. Further, "weight-bearing" exercise, like brisk walking, slows down loss of bone density and helps prevent osteoporosis, if done on a regular basis.

Because keeping to a steady regime of exercise may be difficult, it's a good idea to vary your route as a means of preventing boredom. Perhaps you can walk on level ground for half an hour or so on one day, and walk up and down hills the next day. You might also find a group of like-minded walkers to join, and if there are none, start your own group. All you need is one walking buddy to begin. Just don't let yourself get bored and give up!

Remember that you should make your own decisions about how often and how much to exercise. And, of course, make sure you get a medical checkup before you start any regular exercise program.

Body Weight

At the risk of being shot as the messenger who brings the bad news, I have been told by several professional matchmakers that the most difficult clients to match are those who are overweight. When these individuals are accepted as clients, they are told that they may have to be matched with someone who is also heavy. If you consider yourself seriously overweight and feel that this may be keeping others from making that initial contact, you might consider a weight-loss program that encourages sensible eating and exercise. Consider also the proven fact that those additional pounds can compromise your health.

Even though, according to recent reports, the majority of Americans—60 to 75 percent—weigh more than they should to maintain good health, few of them find other overweight people attractive. I have learned, though, that those few *are* out there, and that some men do prefer heavy women to slender ones, although fewer women appear to prefer heavy men. So far I have interviewed only one man, a widower, who was looking for a *really* heavily built woman, a woman like his late wife whom he had loved deeply. He was disappointed that the chubby women who responded to his newspaper and magazine advertisements, in which he clearly stated his preference, were rarely heavy enough for his taste!

While the search for a truly large woman may be uncommon, several men I have spoken with do talk fondly of women who are "shapely," "zaftig," "curvy," "pleasantly plump," and so on, indicating that skinny women are of little interest to them and that, as one hit film emphasized, "Real Women Have Curves." Rarely, however, do they consider "fat" or "obese" desirable characteristics.

Far more important than how others feel is the way you feel about yourself. If you've always been big and feel comfortable about it, stand tall, hold your head up high, and never doubt your worth! However, if you choose to lose weight, there are a number of excellent weight-loss programs available for you to join. And if group sessions aren't your thing, there are also several proven weight-loss diets to consider—from low-carb to low-fat. Choose the one most appealing and do-able to you. I understand that it may not be easy to shed those extra pounds. But once the weight has been lost, you may find the reward more than worth the effort.

DRESS AND GROOMING

"Ann Landers," "Dear Amy," and other advice columnists frequently publish letters of complaint from women about the slovenliness of men. A "Crabby Road" cartoon reinforcing this idea suggests that women who think about getting remarried should just throw some grubby men's underwear on the floor . . . and presumably they'll think about it again! Not only are husbands reported to be sloppy about their appearance and their living habits, but so are men who are trying to attract a date or a mate.

Men have unfairly gotten a bad rep. They aren't all slobs, even though some see themselves as devastatingly dashing and debonair when they haven't shaved for three days and are wearing a tank top and shorts to take a lady to lunch. Still, the point is worth making. We women generally think we know what men should wear when courting the opposite sex. Problems sometimes arise, though, when we try to choose clothes for ourselves.

Unfortunately, it's not always easy to tell what types of clothes are appropriate, especially as standards are constantly changing. What was once considered well-dressed, may now seem over-dressed. If in doubt, why not simply ask what level of dress is expected at a given event? Are pants acceptable? And must they be dressy, or can they be casual?

New clothes can work wonders in lifting our spirits and boosting our self-confidence, but it is important not to get too carried away by the latest fads and fashions. The trick is to choose what suits you best from among the new styles. Very short skirts can look great on women who have pretty legs—and the nerve to show them off. However, longer, slim-fitting or gently flared skirts may be more attractive if your knees, like mine, are less than perfect. Tights look good on some women, but may be a bit too revealing on others.

Some older women have more generous mid-sections than they once did. Slender skirts worn with slightly fuller tops that tip the hips will draw the eye up, up, and away. This is especially true if there's a colorful scarf or an attractive piece of jewelry at the throat. Some of us used that trick when we were pregnant! It still works.

Very full, floating, or tent-like skirts and tops, rather than conceal, may actually exaggerate a woman's size. A dear friend and colleague recently taped some lectures for television. She was stunned when she viewed the completed video. "I look as though I weigh three hundred pounds!" she complained. While it's true that the camera might have added the appearance of some extra weight, her loose, flowing garments made her look mountainous even though she is shapely and well-proportioned. She now knows that she must wear something a little more form-fitting. If you have access to a digital camera, it might be fun to have someone take pictures of you wearing clothes from your wardrobe.

Just be sure to take a good, brutally honest friend with you when you shop for new outfits!

YOUR FACE AND HAIR

What suited you when you were twenty may not do as much for you now. Even the colors that drew attention to your gorgeous brown eyes and enhanced your creamy skin tones then may not work as well now. Nature—and chemistry, perhaps—have changed the color of your hair, and weather and time have altered the texture of your skin. This has happened gradually.

While you have probably made some changes to your makeup over the years, this may be the time for a critical appraisal of your face and hair. You may decide that you are perfect as you are—in which case, congratulations! Or you may decide on a change so dramatic that your children won't know you if they meet you in the street! Most likely, you will want to make some changes, but remain recognizably yourself.

Makeup and Hairstyles

Relatively inexpensive ways of learning how your appearance might be improved or updated can be found in the department store beauty salon makeover—frequently offered as a "special"—and the photographic glamour shot "transformation."

Beauty salon makeovers sometimes include hair cutting and styling, as well as liberal use of the makeup the technician will encourage you to purchase. Don't feel pressured into buying anything you don't want. Enjoy the experience. The hour or two of personal attention, which sometimes includes a facial, can be relaxing and comforting.

You can make dramatic changes to your appearance by restyling your hair, giving it new highlights, or even changing the color completely. With the help of a good hair stylist, you will emerge with a new, elegant coiffure; some ideas about hair coloring; and probably more makeup on your face than you usually wear, especially in the daytime! You may also pick up some good contemporary makeup tips.

If you take a look at old movies, you'll see how hairstyles change every decade or so. Some of us are stuck in a time warp. We are still wearing our hair as we did in our teens or twenties. Perhaps that style suited our faces then, perhaps it suits our faces *still*, but is it out of fashion? Sometimes it's good to be open to change.

Companies such as Glamour Shots offer photography sessions that are great fun. They can provide valuable information about the most flattering hairstyles, the clothes that enhance a person's best features, and the makeup that conceals blemishes and reveals assets. Their technicians are trained to make clients feel pampered. Finally, you will be shown a slew of pictures of yourself with a range of different looks so you can see how your appearance can be changed. You need not purchase pictures—but you will probably want to! (See Useful Resources on page 169 for photography studio contacts.)

I had a wonderful time at my local Glamour Shots studio! It was not just the hairdo and makeup that changed me so dramatically; it was also the clothing. For my photo shoot, I chose four different outfits from their racks of colorful dresses and suits. I was amused to find that their garments were split up the back, so they'll fit almost anyone. In this way, they can also be put on and taken off without disturbing your new elegant hairstyle. In the course of the photo session, I discovered the flamboyant side of my personality I didn't know existed—a fluffy feather boa and a floppy wide-brimmed hat not being my standard garb! And with the photographer flirting with me so outrageously, I was reduced to giggles and eyelash flutterings that were decidedly out of character, but that made for marvelous pictures!

These makeover photography studios usually offer low-cost "specials" at high school graduation time and before holidays. Don't be afraid to shop around for the best studio and the best deal. Once your photo shoot is complete, you will be shown proofs to select the photos you want. I ordered a set of wallet-sized prints to use for professional purposes—and to include when writing to someone whose personal advertisement asked for a picture. In those pictures, I'm wearing a white tailored jacket with a stand-up collar and silver buttons—a lovely garment that you won't find in my wardrobe!

I love watching the "makeover" programs on talk shows! At one time, celebrity psychologist Dr. Joyce Brothers, with her customary good grace, agreed to be updated on television. The change in her appearance was astonishing, not only because of her new, becoming hairstyle, but also because the stylists exchanged her frumpy, shin-length greenish skirt for a shiny red leather miniskirt that exposed her legs almost to the crotch! She sat next to her daughter—who helped ease her mother's embarrassment by draping *her* long, full skirt over both her own and her mother's legs! Dr. Joyce was transformed into someone marvelously glamorous, but as she said, this look was not for every day!

Cosmetic Surgery

Cosmetic surgery is becoming increasingly commonplace and is no longer reserved for film stars and the very rich—although it is certainly costly. Surgical techniques have been refined to give more "natural" and less obvious results than once was the case. But while cosmetic surgery is thought of as "minor" because no internal organs are involved, it is still serious surgery with all its inherent risks, and should be considered soberly and investigated thoroughly.

Less invasive procedures include injections of Botox to reduce frown lines on the forehead, and injections of collagen to diminish wrinkles around the mouth. While the results of these procedures can be dramatic, they are not long-lasting. They require continuing injections to maintain an improved appearance.

If you expect a face-lift or facial injections to transform your life, you are bound to be disappointed. They will not even transform your face; they will merely make you look a little more "rested" or a bit fresher. Occasionally, I've seen "before and after" pictures of real people (not models), and have found it difficult to see much—or any—real postoperative change. If you are sixty, a face-lift may make you look the best you can look at sixty. It may even make you look five years younger. But it will not make you look thirty, and no reputable surgeon will promise such results.

Some women may consider a particular facial feature so "ugly" that it has caused them embarrassment all their lives. The drooping "wattle" under the chin, the heavy eyelids, or the large nose can cause great misery in our beauty-conscious society. Surgery may make a real difference in those cases. "Beth," a woman in her late sixties, happily married for a third time, recently had neck surgery to remove flesh she had hidden with scarves since her forties. She now proudly wears low-necked blouses to display her newly revealed sleekness! Keep in mind that she did attract three husbands—fleshy neck and all—and that her current husband has always assured her that he loves her as she is.

If you are considering cosmetic surgery, please take the time to perform a thorough investigation. You have only one face and body! Television talk shows present enough evidence of botched faces and distorted breasts to give us pause before committing to the scalpel. You must therefore do your homework. Compare surgeons not only for fees, but far more importantly, for their training.

Call your state medical board about any surgeons on your list. What board certifications does the surgeon hold? More than twenty medical boards offer certification. Be sure that the surgeon is certified by an appropriate medical board. Are there any malpractice suits against him? Beware of slick advertisements. Take time to interview more than one surgeon. How many procedures do they perform each year? The more they do, the better they usually are.

Some people get "hooked" on cosmetic surgery, always expecting that the next procedure will so change them that they will land that super job; find the love of their life; or, more sadly, be able to love themselves. Cosmetic surgery can certainly enhance a person's looks, and can occasionally work miracles. But you will be disappointed if you expect it to push the clock back twenty or thirty years—or even ten years. You should certainly first investigate other much less extreme measures such as professional makeovers and hairstyling!

NOW YOU'RE COOKING!

You have taken some time to assess yourself objectively. You are looking and feeling a bit better—perhaps a lot better—than you did before. That snappy new haircut suits you, and the new tailored outfit minimizes your waistline and encourages you to stand tall. You have a few new items in your wardrobe that are flattering, and that dark blue sweater really brings out the deep blue of your eyes. You've been boning up on your current events, you've become interested in the composition of herbal supplements, and you're learning to play bridge . . .

You are now ready to scan the local newspaper for events geared to your interests. That "salon"—discussion group—on the other side of town seems appealing. You call and speak to the moderator and learn that it promises some interesting conversation among like-minded people. That "mixer" for the fifty-plus crowd might be appropriate. And the walking tour led by the local historical society looks intriguing. Yet you still have doubts. You still feel you aren't ready to meet a lover, a spouse, or that "significant other." You still aren't . . . perfect.

Of course you aren't perfect! The point is, you don't have to be, nor will the person you meet be perfect. Allow yourself to be human and when you meet new people, understand that they are human, too. Very few of us are totally confident about our abilities and our attractiveness when we enter new situations. Trying to make others comfortable with themselves will help you forget what you perceive to be your shortcomings. And take another long look at your list of "good" characteristics!

Two more things. Greet any person of the opposite sex as a new acquaintance, rather than as a prospective lover, and that will help ease the awkwardness. And don't be afraid to be a little *courageous*! The longest journey can only start with the first step.

3

Personal Advertisements and Online Dating

*T*he preparation for this book was certainly a learning experience. In a little over a one-year period, I met and dated more than one hundred men, nearly all in my "preferred" age range of the mid-fifties to the mid- and upper-sixties. Most of them were decent and intelligent; all were nonsmokers. They essentially fell into two groups. Some were looking only for a companion to accompany them to the theater, to the movies, or on walks along the beach. Others had more permanent relationships in mind and were looking for that right someone to enhance their lives—to share more than just an evening of music or dinner. The second group included men who had been long-married and who declared that marriage was their natural state.

Several of the men I met took more than a fleeting interest in me. I formed solid friendships with a handful of them, have felt a bit more than friendship for one or two, and, as I hinted in my preface, accepted one as my husband.

The bumper-sticker slogan "So many men, so little time" began to take on personal meaning, because far more men were drawn into my "net" than I could possibly meet. After all, I had a house, a garden, and a car to maintain; work responsibilities and deadlines to meet; children to keep in touch with; letters to write to family and friends; and on and on.

Friends graciously assure me that I'm "quite nice looking"—whatever that means—but I am quite aware that I am not a great beauty; heads don't turn as I walk by. I am over sixty and not getting any younger. The question, then, is how did I do it? Where *are* all those eligible older men?

Let me assure you, they do exist. The task is to find them and meet them. Meet a *lot* of them until this new situation feels comfortable and you can act naturally and be yourself.

Because this book grew out of my own need to know about today's dating climate, I'll retrace some of my own experiences so you can see how nervous I was, how I was occasionally embarrassed and made to feel foolish. I'll also give you suggestions on how you might avoid some of the minor humiliations I endured! You'll see what worked best for me, and what didn't work at all. And I'll offer some options that might suit people whose interests and requirements differ from mine.

I was terribly naïve at first, shy and self-conscious. I giggled a great deal, which may be charming in one's teens but is not particularly endearing in maturity. Even though I have served in professional capacities for a long time and am used to meeting people in boardrooms and classrooms, the last time I had dated was more than forty years before—and even then, I found meeting boys uncomfortable and awkward! This was an entirely different time and place. I had no idea what to expect—and I didn't know the rules.

PERSONAL ADVERTISEMENTS

I have never cared much for spectator sports, but I do love to walk. A friend to whom I had talked about perhaps joining a walking or hiking group, gave me a copy of *The Southern Sierran*, a publication of the local Sierra Club. Among the personal advertisements, I found this:

> *Handsome SWM [single, white male], young 66, hiker, N\S\D [non-smoker, non-drinker] 5'9". Seeks caring younger SWF. Photo. Box 1234.*

My researcher's blood stirred. I was "younger" and a "single white female." So I answered it. It would be an adventure.

My snapshot and note—on which I put my office address—drew a response with a photograph (snapped at some reunion) of the "handsome SWM," with his arm around singer Pia Zadora. He wore a Jimmy Carter grin, but his face, close to Ms. Zadora's, was jowly, loose skinned, puffy-eyed. I had not the slightest urge to meet him, but, in the interest of research, I gave him a call.

He seemed pleased to hear from me and spoke to me for a long time about his hobbies and his hiking. He advertised regularly in the personal columns and "knew the ropes." When I told him I had never done this before, he snapped back, "That's what they all say!" We arranged to meet in the cafeteria of the county museum of art.

I recognized him from his photo, even without the ear-to-ear grin. He looked tired and his features drooped slightly. His eyes avoided mine when we shook hands; he seemed ill at ease, despite his considerable experience in meeting women this way. Perhaps he had once been handsome, but Box 1234 was not actually hiking these days and was getting stout. His hobby was, or had been, photography, and he brought some expertly matted prints with him—pictures taken years, perhaps decades, before.

Reading Advertisement "Codes"

Lesson Number One: Recognize the codes in advertisements and know how to read them! "Younger" probably means "young." "Active" may mean "be in good shape or don't bother."

Usually, a "legend" accompanies the personal advertisement pages. Some abbreviations, like the ones Box Number 1234 used, are fairly easy to make out. Here are a few of the most common codes:

Marital status: **D** (Divorced), **S** (Single), **W** (Widow[er])

Sex: **F** (Female), **M** (Male)

Religion: **C** (Christian), **J** (Jewish)

Ethnicity or Race: **A** (Asian), **B** (Black), **H** (Hispanic), **W** (White)

Sexual Preference: **G** (Gay), **L** (Lesbian)

Other abbreviations may require a bit of thought. For example:

ISO (in search of)

LTR (long-term relationship)

If you live in a large city, advertisers may include their residential area, such as **WS** (West Side) or **OC** (Orange County). The newspaper or magazine will carry explanations of these codes. Occasionally, an advertiser will make up his own abbreviations. I puzzled for a long time over **SOH**, and learned it meant "sense of humor" only when I asked the man directly.

The museum exhibit was fascinating, but I came away from the meeting saddened, not for myself, but for this man. He needed to hold on to the illusion that somewhere out there was a woman thirty or forty years his junior who was waiting to be bowled over and bedded. As it turned out, "younger" in his advertisement meant a *lot* younger. He told me the most recent "girl" in his life had been twenty-eight years old. Startled, I uttered these words which I realized were rude as soon as I heard them hanging in the air—"Why would any young person want . . . ?"

Newspaper and Magazine Personals

Once unthinkable for "respectable folks," personal advertisements in city and local newspapers and in various magazines provide a major dating resource. It was through personal advertisements that I met most of the one hundred men I dated in my research. And it was through a personal advertisement that I met, although somewhat indirectly, the dear man who is now my husband.

I can't bear to keep you in suspense any longer!

When my book was almost ready to go into typesetting, I decided to advertise once again in a couple of magazines that had yielded rich results. I wanted to be sure that they still could bear fruit before I recommended them, so I inserted personal advertisements in *The Nation,* a politically left-of-center weekly, and *The New York Review of Books,* a weekly that draws a somewhat academic readership.

Again, my advertisements brought several letters from seemingly interesting respondents, so I felt safe in including the two publications in my list of resources. By that time, I was pretty well "dated out" and had no wish to meet any more men for a while!

Some weeks had passed when I received a letter via *The New York Review of Books.* It began: "Perhaps you'd accept this description through another woman's eyes." It then went on to paint a picture in words of Clark, a tall and slender, vibrant but shy man with pale blue eyes and a shock of snow white hair. The letter concluded: "No, he does not know that I am talking him up, but yes, I'll be telling him as soon as this letter hits the mailbox." The writer was the wife of one of Clark's friends. She knew he would never submit an advertisement for himself, but she also knew he had been lonely since his divorce. She wanted to give him a helping hand!

Because Clark's interests matched mine in so many particulars—and because he lived only a few miles from my home—I couldn't help calling the number the person provided. My call was picked up by his answering machine, and he phoned me back later that evening. We talked for more than two hours and arranged to meet for coffee a few days later at Borders.

I should insert here that a week or so prior to this, I'd had dinner with a man I had met once before. When he saw me to my car after the meal, he leaned forward to kiss me. My involuntary reaction was to back away. He was obviously offended, and I drove away feeling terrible about having hurt the man's feelings.

When Clark, who was seated in the cafe, stood up, hand outstretched to greet me, the first thought that popped into my head was, "Now there's a man I wouldn't mind kissing!" Well, we've been kissing ever since.

Personal advertisements are still to be found in the *The Nation* and *The New York Review of Books,* as well as in many *Senior Life* publications, some newspapers and special interest magazines, and newsletters of certain religious and ethnic groups. They will probably never be entirely phased out, but they are gradually being supplanted by online dating services. Still, advertisements in the print media remain a useful resource, especially for those who do not have Internet access or are uncomfortable about going online.

Meeting a Friend Through the Personals

For their sheer wit, I have long scanned the advertisements in *The New York Review of Books*:

Man with superb legs seeks woman with superb bosom . . .

*Rajasthan? Turkey? Ecuador? This fall? DWF, light 50s,
looking for Man (5'9", 40–60) who wants to go on these
and other journeys through life. Be happy. Be solvent,
and we'll be on our way.*

And one written tongue-in-cheek—or I hope so!

*Male professor, late nineties, alert many afternoons, seeks
vibrant beauty in forties, preferably with nursing skills.*

I wonder how many responses that one brought! Most of the advertisers are based in New York, but one read:

Retired professor seeks intelligent, shapely woman to share conversation, nature, arts, travel. Los Angeles.

"Retired" might mean *recently* retired—someone of, say, sixty-five or sixty-six? I took courage and called the number listed. Most people list a box number, but this man's home number was given. I mentioned my recent widowhood on his answering machine and left my telephone number.

My husband had been dead less than a year, but I learned that this man was even more newly bereft than I was. His wife had been killed by a hit-and-run driver only five months before as he and his wife crossed the street. A mathematician, he told me he'd been retired for two years, which I supposed meant he was about sixty-seven. We would have lunch the following day at a well-known neighborhood restaurant. He arrived exactly on time, a beanpole of a man, so tall he seemed to veer slightly to one side. He looked frail—small wonder, given his circumstances—but after a while, his personality shone through. He was a nice, funny man—in terrible emotional pain.

Back at my house after lunch—my daughter was at home that day, so I felt comfortable inviting him to my home to continue our conversation—he promptly asked if he could put his head down for a while! A sign of his age and emotional state, perhaps? I took him to the guest room, gave him a pillow, and went off to write letters.

He awoke refreshed and in no hurry to leave, so we sat in the garden until evening, with him planning to come back early the next day to walk around Hollywood Lake with me. At last, he left, but not before giving me a big hug at the bottom of the steps. It felt good—the first hug I'd had for a long time. A fine and decent man, I thought, but I was troubled by his years. By now, I was estimating that he was somewhere in his mid-seventies.

My daughter and I talked together about the importance of age. She dismissed it as a non-issue. "What counts, Mum, is physical and emotional age, not the number of years a person has lived." Of course she was right. We all know a few "old men" in their forties. If a person is active, in good health, living for today and thinking about tomorrow and the next day, his chronological age becomes less important.

The mathematician had a fascinating past, having worked on the development of the atomic bomb. Like a schoolgirl, I hung on his every word as he talked of the famous physicists he'd known—Fermi, Oppenheimer, Feynman—and of the ethical problems he'd had with nuclear power.

After several outings with him to the beach and the movies and a concert, I thought I could really get to like this man. But with my gradual warming came his increasing depression. So soon after his tragedy, it was just too early for a new relationship. His depression deepened and, in empathy, my spirits dropped too, as I was reminded of my own loss. I decided that this was not good for me, and that we would remain just casual friends.

That friendship, which is now deep and solid, has sustained us both through some trying times. Good friends are precious, so don't overlook the possibility that while the person you meet may not turn out to be the man of your romantic dreams, he may widen your circle of friends and enrich your life.

The Mechanics of Personal Advertisements

A measure of safety is built into personal ads, because you have the choice of using a box number. This allows the newspaper or magazine to mail responses to you, so you need not divulge any identifying information until and unless you are ready to do so. You will also have the opportunity to screen men prior to meeting them by talking on the telephone—at length and often, if you wish. For extra assurance, you should make sure that your first meeting is in a public place, and you should not invite a stranger into your home until you are sure that he poses no danger to you. And you shouldn't let that wonderful Mary Higgins Clark mystery novel *Loves Music, Loves to Dance* deter you! In that book, a serial murderer finds his victims through newspaper personals. While this made for an exciting story, if you are sensible and cautious, you are in no more danger from a person you meet through a personal advertisement than you are from a person you meet in any other way.

The mechanics of using personal advertisements vary from one medium to another. Most magazines and newspapers charge by the word and give a small discount for multiple insertions. In major magazines, the cost can be more than five dollars per word, with an extra fee for handling and forwarding replies.

Of course, you can choose to include your telephone number or your e-mail address in your advertisement. Respondents can contact you more quickly this way than by writing via a box number. But if you request a photograph, only a letter will do.

SOME SAMPLE PERSONALS

These personals may give you a taste of the kinds of advertisements placed by some over-fifties in various personals pages—and give you some ideas for developing your own.

Women Seeking Men

Symphony, science, art, and having coffee with you. Sweet, pretty, prof(essional) DJF seeks educ affectionate N\S WM 50's.

Outstanding, outgoing, outrageous, upstanding, upbeat, upfront, uproarious, introspective, innately intimate. Interested? Mid-life woman seeks matching (left-leaning, right-brained) man.

Wanted, a special 56–60 WM who still likes Disneyland, old movies, dancing slow, the family, and grandchildren.

Serve and volley with this dynamic, slim, attractive DBF. Meet me at the net, the theater, the beach, or the movies if you are an active, quality SBM, 50–60, ready to follow through in a romantic game of singles or doubles.

Grandma looking for grandpa. Must be 60+. Please give me a call.

Take a chance, Life's a gamble, anyway, and you might win the heart of a large, good-hearted lady. U: 50–65 with same qualities.

Classy chassis, low mileage\hi performance. SF loaded with extras. Romantically designed 4 SM, fin-sec (financially secure). 50–64.

Faithful Penelope longs for her Odysseus; beautifully, artfully, joyously, patiently waiting 4 the love that endures . . .

Outstandingly beautiful, marvelous, charming, and above all modest DF ISO n\s companion.

Men Seeking Women

1938 New Yorker, well maintained like 58 model, trim, white, 66, grt lks (looks) and body style. Lifetime warranty.

Retired college professor, SWM, special, sks loving intel shapely lady. 55–65 for mutual life enhancement.

Attractive fit DWM, 57, smoker, likes travel, romantic evenings, ISO slim, attractive WF lifemate to 63.

61, witty, lover of movies, music, animals and travel. Seeks slim N\S lady to 55 to share life.

Grow old disgracefully. Celebrate the delights. DWM 59. N\S.

Widower, 65+, Christian Scientist. ISO one with same understanding.

Caring SWM. 60, engineer. Enjoys art, good music. ISO SWF, 50–56, trim, ready for romantic monog(amous) rel(ationship).

Many personals columns also list "Men Seeking Men" and "Women Seeking Women"—so there's something for everyone.

Placing My Own Advertisements

As I had made a good friend by responding to an advertisement in *The New York Review of Books,* I inserted my own personal, giving a box number and requesting a photograph. It drew three responses. I had stipulated fifty-five to sixty-five as the age range of interest, but two of the respondents turned out to be substantially older. One, who was interesting on paper, had been a music critic and was particularly knowledgeable about chamber music, one of my passions. He described himself as "handsome" and invited me to a concert.

By no stretch of the imagination could "George" be called handsome. The rather blurred snapshot he had sent me was either of someone else or had been taken a long time ago. We got off to a rough start, as he got lost on his way to our meeting place. He then got lost on the way to the concert hall, causing us to miss the entire first half of the program. Once at the concert, he spoke to me only occasionally as he knew several people in the crowd, hailed them noisily, and held them captive with stories of who was playing what music—while I stood on the fringes, wishing I was somewhere else. Finally, he did introduce me to some of his acquaintances, all of them charming and almost any one of whom I would rather have been with that evening! On the way back, he got lost a third time. We drove back in relative silence, knowing we would not meet again.

Another respondent to my advertisement met me for coffee at a beach restaurant. He spoke of himself as "the most reluctant bachelor around." Sophisticated Italian-born "Luigi" was blasé about the dating scene. He had been on the "quest" for a partner for a very long time. He had waited until he was forty-two to wed, and was divorced after only eight years of marriage. Now in his upper sixties, he was wary about another commitment.

When I spoke of my full life and my good fortune in having the support of friends and family, he indicated that he had heard all these phrases before and saw them as "codes." His response was sharp: "Perhaps you don't need to venture out, given such a full life!"

Luigi and his male friends were experienced at dating through the personals, and he confirmed my observations about the way people described themselves.

"The men all advertise themselves as younger than they really are. They say they are taller and better-looking than they really are. You have to get the women to meet you before you can impress them—but a woman has to be disappointed in the reality," he said.

"Perhaps that *is* the reality for them," I suggested, noting that, despite his protestations about the foolishness of lying, he had understated his own age.

Luigi called me a few weeks later, charming and courtly. He didn't want me to think he hadn't liked me but "a lady from long ago" had returned to his life. He was eager to tell me that I was "Lovely! Perfect!," and urged me to keep meeting people and having fun. He may, or may not, have been telling the truth about the lady from the past. I later learned from some of my interviewees that this is a fairly common device used, mostly by women, to gently let down men they don't want to see any more!

As the return from *The New York Review of Books* ad was a bit sparse,

I placed an advertisement in *The Nation,* a magazine to which I had long subscribed. It, too, is published in New York with a national circulation appealing to those who are politically left of center and relatively intellectual. Here, I struck the mother lode! The response was overwhelming; some twenty men answered, including three PhDs and two MDs. Most were from my city, as I had given my hometown in the advertisement, but a few were from other parts of the state, and one was even from the East Coast.

I did as Luigi had suggested. I met most of them and had such a hectic social life that I hardly got any work done!

The Nation was such a good resource that I couldn't wait to tell my older, single women friends. Two of them placed personal advertisements and had responses similar to mine. In fact, a few of the same men who'd written to me also wrote to them!

It's fun to recall being wooed with fruit by one of *The Nation* men! A university colleague, enchanted when she heard about it, asked: "Does he bring you mangoes and guavas and exotic things like that?" "No," I said. "Just citrus; it isn't a metaphor for anything. It's just fruit."

The "fruit man" did, in fact, propose marriage—over the top of a bag of grapefruits. It was the first serious proposal I'd had and I seriously considered it—for about a minute and a half. It took me only that long to realize that I was too recently widowed to make such a commitment. Also, I was having too interesting a time to settle down just yet!

The number of responses to personal advertisements and the suitability of respondents will vary from advertisement to advertisement. Some men I have interviewed tell me they are sometimes swamped with a hundred calls or more. At other times, only three or four women will respond. Some of my advertisements in our local newspaper have yielded ten or twelve responses, while others have brought only one or two—or none. So don't take it personally or feel you're a "failure" if your advertisement doesn't draw many—or any—responses. The success rate seems to vary randomly for everyone, and you may have more responses to the next advertisement you place.

The men who have answered have included a newly widowed, internationally famous psychiatrist—an instantly recognizable name in academic circles; a building contractor; a hairdresser; a university professor; a physician-artist; a union organizer; several businessmen; and many retired men from a wide range of professions.

Iris's Story

One of my friends, "Iris," is now seriously involved with a man she met through *The Nation's* personal column. The two are talking of marriage as he prepares to move to the West Coast from an eastern city. They began their courtship through the mail and long cross-country telephone calls. Even before they met face to face, they felt a real affinity for each other. Finally, "Louis" traveled to Los Angeles for a long weekend, staying at a hotel near Iris's apartment.

The romance blossomed quickly, both of them feeling the pressure of the geographical distance between them and the need to make the most of every moment together. After Louis visited twice more, he decided to move across the country. The old cliché applies: Love can overcome obstacles, even courtship across three thousand miles.

FOLLOWING UP ON A PERSONAL AD

Before you decide to meet a respondent in person, you should first talk to him on the telephone. Your telephone conversation will help you decide whether you would like to know him better.

The Initial Telephone Meeting

Once you've responded to a personal ad, or someone has responded to yours, the telephone call is the first filter of the screening process. Now you can talk as long as you wish at relatively little cost, gathering a fair amount of information about him and deciding if you want to meet him.

The safest areas to ask about are work and hobbies, where he grew up, and where he went to school. You can also ask about his tastes in music and the arts, about his children, and so on.

If you like, you can probe a little into his marital history, although some tact is needed here. People may take offense at being asked really personal questions like, "Have you been involved in any relationships since becoming single?" A rule of thumb is to ask yourself how *you* would feel if you were asked that kind of question. Nevertheless, you will want to know if the man is still angry or bitter about a divorce or if he is grieving deeply. You might want to be sure that he is, indeed, unattached romantically!

You will also want to try to discern if he is basically a cheerful, forward-looking person or a grouch. Does he drone on and on about himself, or does he seem genuinely interested in knowing about you? In short, is this a person with whom you would like to spend some time?

Sometimes, the initial telephone "meeting" is so delightful that it continues for an hour or more. The two of you may develop a real rapport and look forward to meeting in person. But he is still a blind date and you may—or may not—be disappointed in the flesh-and-blood reality. It's an adventure! And all that is lost is a little of your time.

From time to time, you'll speak to someone who may have had a terrible day and who projects all his frustrations on you! "Jack" left a message for me. I called back, only to find him so touchy as to make pleasant conversation impossible.

"What kind of work do you do?" I asked—a usual and, you'd think, fairly nonthreatening question.

"I'm an art teacher."

"That's wonderful!" I said, genuinely interested. "Where do you teach?"

For some reason, this question made him angry.

"What does it matter where I teach?" he snapped. "Would I be more loveable if I taught at Harvard than if I taught at some other place?"

"I'm sorry," I said. "Where you teach isn't really significant. It's just that I teach, too, and I thought we might teach at the same place."

When I said I had been happily married, he came back with, "The longer you're a widow, the more wonderful and saintly your husband will become. I know these things."

Straining to be polite, I talked a little about my work and interests.

"If you have such a rich life," he said, "why are you advertising for a man?"

Exasperated, I suggested that he was obviously tired of responding to these kinds of questions and seemed to have a bit of a chip on his shoulder.

That made him *really* angry. "How rude of you! How rude! All you have to say is that you don't think we have much in common and good-bye."

"Okay," I sighed. "I don't think we have much in common, Jack. Good-bye."

As I hung up the phone, feeling rather mean, I realized that I should have excused myself from the encounter earlier. Instead of trying to deal with this man's odd responses to what I thought were reasonable questions, I should have protected myself from the discomfort he caused me and from the wasted effort of making conversation that was going nowhere. So if you ever find yourself in a similar situation, you might remind yourself that you don't have to serve as psychoanalyst to clearly troubled people!

The First Meeting

A first meeting with a stranger—and the man *is* a stranger, even if you've spoken on the telephone many times and feel as though you know him—should be in a public place with other people around. Most people choose to meet for coffee at a coffee house or restaurant that one of you knows well, or one that is easily reached by both of you. The advantage of the coffee meeting is that it can be brief—but need not be—and a cup of coffee is a minor expenditure compared to a luncheon or dinner.

Usually, these meetings take place mid-morning. If both people are working during the day, they may choose to meet for lunch at a centrally placed restaurant. If they work in different parts of the city, coffee on a Saturday or Sunday morning may be the answer. This is clearly something to be worked out for the convenience of both people involved.

Be prepared for the first meeting to be the last. You may simply not like the look of the person, he may not be taken with you, or you may be mutually disappointed. On the other hand, you may become so engrossed with each other's conversation that morning coffee stretches into lunch into dinner—and then the movies.

I have had both kinds of experiences. One man I met for morning coffee got down to brass tacks immediately.

"I must have sex with any new woman within two weeks; there's no point in wasting time. The sex has to be right or there's no point in continuing. Time is not on my side."

Seeing my horrified expression, he told me I would never get married if I wasn't prepared to "live life." "You'll still be looking in ten years time and every day, the merchandise is losing value! All you'll be able to find will be old men who are ill!" He was equally outspoken about the need to "keep the juices flowing" by having sex. "Use it or lose it!"

Feeling physically nauseated by his hateful words, I jumped up from the table, uneaten croissant in hand, ran to my car, and sped off as fast as I could!

This, I told myself, is one of the "jerks" they keep telling me is out there!

Fortunately, few of the men I met were jerks. Most were well-mannered and pleasant, and even if we didn't arrange another meeting, we spent an enjoyable hour or two in good conversation. Chapter 6 gives details about safety precautions you should be sure to take.

First Meeting Talk

Men tell me that the conversation at that first meeting is better if it doesn't get too personal. "She told me she'd been clinically depressed and had tried to commit suicide on three occasions. Honestly, I did not need to know that! Not yet. Then, she asked me if I'd like her to go home with me. I didn't think so! I've got too many knives and things around . . ."

It is probably not a good idea to talk about your ex-husband or the circumstances of your divorce at this early stage. I must confess that I am put off right away when a man starts bad-mouthing his ex-wife, so I can see that men might feel the same way.

Other topics best avoided when you first meet—and these include recommendations given to me by several professional matchmakers— are your health problems, your financial problems, your bothersome workplace disputes, serious worries about your children, and your longing to be married! We all know that upbeat people are much more fun to be with than complainers, so keep it light.

This meeting is an opportunity for you to get to know enough about the man to see if you care to meet him again, and to present yourself in a positive way. That doesn't mean you must play-act or pretend to be someone you are not. Listen as much as you talk. Expand on your earlier telephone conversation. Ask the man where he grew up. Does he like his job? Has he traveled recently? What kinds of films does he prefer? Does he have children? Let him tell you about them, if he wants to.

It is always a little awkward to make conversation with someone you haven't met before, but if you are alert to what is going on in the world, you will find something to talk about: the latest hit movie; the Oscars; the Emmys; current happenings; the latest food fads; books; sports. Glance through the morning newspaper or the latest news magazine for some ideas before you set off for the meeting, just in case you run out of topics.

Both of you may be nervous, trying so hard to make a good impression that you babble on and on. You don't have to tell your entire life story right now. Nor do you have to take any of this too seriously. It's just coffee, not an emotional commitment!

Who Pays? The New Etiquette

As a professional, I am used to paying my own way. Dinner with colleagues, male or female, usually means splitting the bill, with no one feeling uncomfortable about it. But what do you do when meeting a man for the first time over lunch or a snack? The offer to pay for yourself is sometimes received gratefully, as lots of people are living on fixed incomes and eating out is a luxury. Most often, the offer is dismissed with a wave of the hand and, "No, I wouldn't hear of it!"

Once, when I told my lunch companion that I was conducting research for a book on dating in later life—as I usually did at some point during a first meeting—he became indignant. "I never allow a lady to pay for her meal, but if this is business for you, it's quite legitimate!" Fair enough.

Sure that I would never hear from him again, I was surprised when, some four months later, he called. "I hope you've finished work on your book by now. I would really like to see you again, but I don't want to be one of your research subjects." I had to look through my notes to remind myself who he was! By the way, he insisted on paying for dinner the next time—and for the theater as well.

Most of the men I met were fascinated with my research topic and eager to relate their experiences as "singles." They usually bought lunch, too! They told me that it is unusual for women to offer to pay their way, but that they do appreciate it when it happens, even if they don't accept. Not only do most women not offer to share the food tab, but there are some who turn men off with their extravagant demands. A nice fellow, with whom I shared Sunday brunch at the beach, told me of a woman who chided him about the restaurant he had chosen. "Honestly, it was a good eatery, but she complained 'You could have taken me *anywhere*; what made you pick this place?'" You can bet he never asked her out again.

Men do not like to feel they are being taken advantage of. A dear old friend, who had been looking for the "right lady" for some time, often shared some of the details of his dates with me. He arranged to meet a woman at noon. "I don't bother with first meetings for coffee any more," he said. "Might as well have lunch. It seems more substantial, somehow." The woman, who happened to be French, insisted that they eat at a French restaurant she knew. "John," my friend, was agreeable. Then he saw the menu—and the exorbitant prices!

"I couldn't believe what she ordered. The most expensive dish she could find—and a daiquiri before the meal, and an elaborate dessert afterwards. I didn't like her much, anyway, and I could see she was aiming to get a super meal at my expense. So I told her we were going Dutch—something I never do. She was really taken aback, but she paid up!"

Who pays for what requires negotiation these days; the old rules of etiquette apply some, but not all of the time. Young people and business people take sharing costs for granted, whereas some older women tell me, "A real gentleman pays to take a lady out." You have to use your judgment and a measure of tact.

Love at First Sight

Forget it! That's my sincere recommendation to you. I hear lots of talk about chemistry and electricity between people as their eyes meet across a crowded room. Yes, people can take an instant liking to each other, but don't be disappointed—and don't give up on the person—if that chemistry doesn't make itself felt at a first meeting. Indeed, if there are flashes of lightning when you shake hands, be prepared for the storm to fizzle out pretty quickly.

For your own sake, please be realistic about this. Don't let someone walk away just because that initial spark is missing. He may be perfect for you if you just give him a chance.

USING PERSONALS TO ORGANIZE SINGLES EVENTS

An interesting way of using personal advertisements is to invite single people in your preferred age group to a mix-and-match gathering, party, or evening out. Here is an actual advertisement from a recent New York magazine:

> *We are 7 women looking for 7 men to join us for a dinner party. We are as diverse and as interesting as we'd like each of you to be. We are, and are looking for men who are, fun-*

*loving, 50 plus, attractive, intelligent, emotionally
healthy, financially secure, non-smokers with a sense
of humor. Individuals please send photo with note.*

These advertisers made very clear the kinds of men they were looking for. Letters and photographs were requested to help screen the
respondents. Almost surely, they used follow-up phone calls before
making their final selection.

Given seven men and seven women who begin with some interests
in common, the chances are good that some of them will find agreeable
matches. At the very least, they'll all have an enjoyable evening and a
good meal!

If you can't find six women friends prepared to help you organize a
dinner party, think of other kinds of evening or afternoon events. These
could be concert or theater outings for, say, three men and three women . . .

An ad in the "Mutual Interests" or the "50 Plus" section of the personals pages might find the appropriate men and women to make up
the group. An advertisement taken directly from my local paper reads as
follows: "Single golfer seeking other single golfers to fill out some four-
somes on 18 hole courses." Another suggests organizing a group of men
and women to attend a museum together, followed by a meal at a
nearby restaurant. Docent-led tours, which are regularly scheduled at
most major museums, provide a good framework for this kind of activity. Other advertisers seek "like-minded men and women to get together
at coffee houses and other venues to listen to, or play, acoustic music" or
"on-fire M/F Christians, any race, for prayers, discussions, and Bible
study." The possibilities are limited only by your imagination.

MEETING ONLINE

Who would have thought, even quite recently, that millions of people
would be looking for love online? Yet other types of online services have
been with us for many years. You can buy airline tickets, pay your bills,
send faxes, e-mail letters, book your vacations, take university courses,
and research the stock market on your computer. So why not search for
romance on the computer, too?

My friend, "Holly," who's in her fifties, met the man she has been
seeing for the past eighteen months via the Internet, and one of *her*
friends is marrying her cyberspace "match" next month. Even Rush

Limbaugh, the conservative political commentator, met his third wife online. This wave of the future has been here for quite a while!

For those who aren't familiar with these electronic advances, all of this seems pretty scary. Yet *The New York Times* business section, on one of its "Bulletin Boards," states that the total of "unique visitors" to the top online dating services is nearly 25 million per month!

If you are already online, the following information will be familiar to you. It is offered here to give courage to those who have yet to get their feet wet. Of course, you will need a computer with a modem. This will at least allow you to access your online service by plugging into a telephone line.

Most online services carry a monthly charge. This fee will usually give you unlimited time online, which you will surely need if you plan to use online dating services. Several online services are free, and some are fairly low in cost—although that usually reflects only a limited number of hours. Online services are changing so rapidly that it is difficult to predict which arrangements will still be available in the future.

You can "meet" people online just as you meet them through personal advertisements in newspapers and magazines. First, you use an online dating service to look for people who share your interests and values. When you start communicating, you are, according to those who use these services, "inside each other's head." Many cyberspace users find that their online friends are much easier to talk to than people who are in the same room. The medium allows an outpouring of heart and soul that is less possible in ordinary meeting places. This is probably attributable to each person's hiding behind an onscreen "name"— remaining truly anonymous. "I can't believe I'm telling you this. I've never talked about this to anyone before," is the kind of statement often made online.

It's easy, after communicating for a period of time, to "fall in love." You are, of course, falling in love with an image—or rather, a "mind merge." It's most probably a fantasy, which may simply disappear when you meet in person. Or perhaps it won't.

Phyllis's Story

"Phyllis," a woman who met her fiancé online, found even speaking on the telephone to "Ian" a strange and unnerving experience after having communicated with him only through the computer.

"Ian is really 'strong' when he talks online. When he speaks in person, though, he is much . . . meeker. It was a difficult transition."

Ian lived on the West Coast; Phyllis, in New York. The two arranged to meet in New York three months after having had their first computer conversation.

"We really knew a great deal about each other." Phyllis told me. "We had told each other more than most people say in a lifetime." Still, had the two met in any other way, she says, it's unlikely they would have given each other the time of day. Ian is a smoker; Phyllis hates everything about cigarettes. Phyllis is tall; Ian is short. Ian says he would have been intimidated by Phyllis—a successful, independent professional—if he hadn't had the opportunity to get "inside her head" before he met her.

Ian has now relocated to a small town on the edge of New York, and commutes to visit Phyllis. He has reduced his smoking to only a couple of cigarettes a day, and hopes to give them up completely before the two marry.

ABOUT ONLINE DATING SERVICES

There are hundreds of online dating sites available to you. Membership costs vary, and can range from as little as thirteen dollars a month to more than fifty dollars a month. Prices will undoubtedly change over time, but a month of even the most expensive service will probably continue to cost less than a single insertion of a personal advertisement in an upscale magazine.

The dating sites are all similar in the way they work, but each is distinctive in some respects. Some, for instance, cater to people with specific interests, such as art, music, or politics. Useful Resources on page 169 provides a list of the most popular online dating services, including some sites for people with special interests.

Some sites will allow you to browse through their offerings at no charge so you can see the range of available single men or women in your specified age group and geographical area. You can often stipulate a given number of miles from your home as your dating range. Usually, you will see a "profile" of each man or woman and, in many cases, a photograph. Some people prefer not to post a picture but, to judge by some of my interviewees, this has not deterred the interest of prospective dates.

Spence's Story

"Spence," a man close to sixty, feels that a person's looks are misleading or irrelevant when seeking a serious mate. He has recently married a woman he met through Yahoo. Neither had seen a picture of the other before they met in person, although by that time, they were pretty sure they were in love.

Spence began his search for a mate with a one-month subscription to an online dating service at a low introductory price. After that first month, he renewed his membership for another three months. During that time, he received fifty-four inquiries and actually met ten of the women. He was interested in meeting only those women who were close to his own age, as he found younger women shallow and less serious.

Spence feels that people should be wary about giving out personal information too soon after meeting online. "It's dangerous out there," he claims, "and ladies weren't as cautious as I was. Some were a bit cavalier about their safety." To show that he was who he purported to be, he showed his dates his driver's license but covered his address. "Some of them looked at me strangely."

Besides liking the anonymity of corresponding online, Spence found advantages in communicating through writing. "When you meet face to face, there's body language. Stuff gets in the way. Online, though, there's no inflection, no voice. Just pure thought. You have an indication of what's in their heads from their writing."

One disadvantage of online dating, Spence says, is the time it takes to sift through the possibilities and to respond to messages. "I was sitting at the computer for four or five hours a day, trying to keep up with the correspondence." He also feels that the instant two-way connection made possible by e-mail has its problems, as it can lead very quickly to feelings of love. "Five ladies declared they had fallen in love with me within a week. We hadn't met and I hadn't posted a picture. It's all in the mind. A fantasy."

Spence and his wife had been married for less than a year when I interviewed him, and they still lived some miles apart while they negotiated a move to a shared household. They are so taken with instant messaging that they still communicate that way every day. In fact, Spence is considering continuing this mode of communication even when they live together—with computers in separate rooms. "With talking this way, information given off by facial expressions and voice tone is omitted, information that can be misconstrued or misunderstood. It's especially helpful in case of disagreements."

Kenneth's Story

"Kenneth," an energetic and youthful-looking man in his late seventies, only recently added online capability to his computer, and is enthusiastic about online dating. "The web has opened it up for older people," he says.

Kenneth signed on first with Matchmaker.com, and then with Match.com. He was looking for a woman who loves the wilderness and hiking, likes to swim, and is sophisticated, tall, and cultured.

Ken explained that members of these online dating services are required to post "profiles"—basically, personal advertisements in which they describe their own attributes as well as the attributes of their ideal mate. Kenneth told me that he put himself in the sixty-five-to-seventy category. "I'll strike out if I put my real age." He says women cheat, too. "One woman used a picture that was twenty years old." He now asks directly, "How old are your photographs?"

Kenneth says that Match offers an advantage over Matchmaker, in that it allows you to insert a key word, and then finds a match for whom that key word is also important. His key word is "hiking." Matchmaker, on the other hand, allows more space to write a good essay.

Many services ask each member to describe their ideal first date. Kenneth says that many women write about a wonderful meal in a lovely restaurant on the beach. He doesn't respond to those. Confirming other respondents' views, he draws the line on women who are "meal scroungers" and who never offer to share the cost or cook a meal even after several dinners out.

Unlike Spence, Kenneth put several pictures of himself online, and likes to see pictures of the women, as well. Chronological age is not important to him, but he does look for a "feminine" woman with beautiful qualities.

When Kenneth telephoned me only a couple of weeks after our first interview, he had met the woman with whom he hoped to spend the rest of his life. When he realized that he was interested in her, he had to "fess up" to having misrepresented his age by ten years. The lady, who is sixty, was at first terribly disappointed by both the fact that he had lied and the age difference. "If I had told you my real age, you wouldn't have been interested in me—and we wouldn't have met," he explained. This was true, the lady admitted. After only a few meetings, age became irrelevant and the two seem destined to be together.

Millicent and Nora

Not everyone is quite as pleased with the online experience. "Millicent," a successful professional woman of fifty-eight, has had several long-term relationships in the fifteen years since her divorce, but has met "no one significant, so far."

Millicent has been using Matchmaker on and off for about a year, and has been disappointed in the caliber of men, feeling that they misrepresent their interests and their intent in their profiles. Her experience is that men in her preferred age range—fifties and sixties—are looking for a younger woman with whom they can have a child. These men do not respond to someone who does not put a photo online, and often lie about their looks and their age. "One man said he was fifty-nine and he turned out to be seventy-four."

"Nora," in her late forties and never married, uses Jdate, which advertises itself as "the world's largest Jewish singles community." She is actively communicating with and meeting "quality men," but finds the process *very* time consuming. "At first," she said, "it looks like a cornucopia. A whole lot of men. But it's like the whole world on a computer. You have to sift through."

She feels that many of the men who seek mates online are socially inept. "They think they have all these women at their fingertips, but these are men who would not otherwise meet lots of women. This one is overweight, this one doesn't make a living. . . . Some of the e-mails are witty and promising but when you get on the phone with the men, you find they are impossible. They talk about themselves, themselves, themselves—a sure sign of desperation."

When asked if she had met anyone promising online, Nora said that she had gone out with a couple of men with whom she could have continued, "But I wasn't it for them. Tough, but that's reality."

My Venture Into Cyberspace

To better understand the experience of looking for love through online dating services, I signed on with Match, Jdate, and Sciconnect. I soon found that, indeed, one is presented with a seeming cornucopia of eligible men. I described myself as seeking a man who lived within a ten-mile range from my home, between fifty-five and seventy-five years of age. In return, I was shown hundreds of possibilities, with and without photographs. Some of the profiles were witty and entertaining, some well-written and inviting:

> *Arrogant, conceited, domineering and demanding. Shall I*
> *go on? Decadent, drunk, and debauched. Are you worthy*
> *of me? Don't be ridiculous. And don't forget to write.*

> *60 year old widower. Practicing law. Settled in my*
> *circumstances. I will wind up my practice soon and turn*
> *to travel and recreation. Political views are liberal and*
> *my religion is nil. Tall and very fit. I read much history*
> *and philosophy and would like to meet someone 50–60*
> *with whom to discuss same.*

> *Retired process engineer. Keen interest in most areas of*
> *science. Fit via running. Non-smoker, considerate, positive.*
> *Enjoy conversation, laughter, hiking, travel, classical music,*
> *dancing, the arts, sports. . . . Seeking woman with sense of*
> *humor, warm-hearted, adventurous.*

Each service offered page after page of profiles. After scanning the first 250 possibilities from Jdate—and there were more—I was so exhausted that I had to pause for a cup of tea! It should be noted that of all the hundreds of men whose profiles I read, only two or three were widowers. Almost all were divorced. Further, contrary to expectations, most of the men sought women in an age range very close to their own. Only one or two of the fifty-five-plus men indicated a preference for younger women.

Online Innovations

According to *The New York Times,* along with the surge in online dating has come the availability of more innovative options. For instance, just as dinner parties can be arranged through personal advertisements, similar gatherings can now be found online. Oprah Winfrey, on one of her programs, introduced an organization called Eight at Eight. This group arranges dinners for four men and four women, matched for age, at restaurants in Atlanta, Chicago, Dallas, Denver, and Las Vegas. The hope of Eight at Eight is to extend the service to other major cities. (See Useful Resources on page 169 for their website.) Similar programs already exist in San Francisco and New York. In addition to making possible matches, participants also meet people of the same sex with whom they can develop friendships. Watch for other interesting developments!

Clearly, the Internet is a useful tool when searching for interesting men, but be prepared to spend many hours separating the wheat from the chaff. Also expect little fibs and tall stories. A final precaution is that some e-mails—from women as well as from men—can get raunchy. The anonymity that offers security also offers license to write of subjects that might not otherwise be mentioned to a stranger. You can, of course, immediately break off communication with anyone you find offensive.

Finally, if you do want to meet someone *off*line—in person—all the same precautions apply as when meeting any stranger. Meet in a public place—and so on.

You've worked your way through a lot of information about making the plunge directly into dating: personal advertisements in newspapers and magazines, organizing your own singles events, and meeting online. Pause and digest. There's more!

4

Dating Services and Other Resources

*G*ood men, it seems, have always been hard to find, but they *are* out there. The ways to look for them are many and varied, direct and indirect. So far, I have suggested that personal advertisements and online dating—very direct methods of looking for compatible members of the opposite sex—work well for many people. Now I'll give you my recommendations—the pros and the cons, based on my experience and research—regarding other direct methods. These include dating services and matchmakers, dances and socials, and singles events, both commercial and noncommercial.

DATING SERVICES AND MATCHMAKERS

Before I became a widow, I hardly noticed the profusion of advertisements for dating and matchmaking services. I had heard about video dating, and I recalled a particularly poignant episode of the 1980s television show *thirtysomething*. Two of the female characters, anxious about the ticking of their biological clocks and eager to marry, sign up to be "video-matched." They giggle with embarrassment as they first perform for the video camera, and then flip through the pages of available men.

Several of these companies have called me and some of my interviewees to offer their services, probably because we have placed advertisements in personal columns. Lists of singles seem to circulate among and between the businesses that cater to this huge group. In Los Angeles, for instance, there are more than 1.5 million unmarried adults; the figures are proportionately high in other cities. My name, it seems, is on several lists.

How Dating and Matchmaking Services Work

One day a woman called me from a singles club offering a video library, a personal library, background checks on clients, and so on. (The term "personal library" refers to books, as opposed to videotapes, filled with photographs of and information about single men and women looking for partners or dates.)

"Come in and look through the videos and the information," she cooed. "You'll feel like a kid in a candy store when you see all the wonderful men you can choose among!"

I'm sure she had no idea of my age. Video dating works best, if it works at all, for younger people. Men who have joined video dating services have told me of their disappointment in the small number of older women who participate. Most older people do not find it particularly appealing to choose partners from a book of photographs or from videotapes. The picture books are filled with pretty young girls and handsome young men, and many older people are uncomfortable with the idea of being judged by their looks, especially when the collections are not categorized by age. Perhaps if some enterprising business people ran a service exclusively for the over-fifties, folks in this age range would be more accepting.

In any case, dating services—which are just what the name says: services that arrange dates, not necessarily matches or marriages—can be expensive. One agency, for instance, charges several hundred dollars a year for a passive membership. The member's picture is entered in the books, and other people have the option of selecting her. The passive member cannot select anyone. The cost of an active membership can begin at well over a thousand dollars—and these charges can change at any time. An active member can pick and be picked from both books and videos.

A "picked" member is sent a card or e-mail indicating that someone is interested in her. She may then decide whether or not to meet the person who made the selection. A visit to the office can provide more information and a look at the interested party's photo and files. As with personal advertisements, the couple will talk on the telephone before planning a meeting.

Matchmakers are of another order, and usually are far more expensive than dating services. Matchmakers claim to find partners—people who want "long term relationships" or marriage—and couples are supposedly individually matched for interests, hobbies, religion, goals and values, age, appearance requirements, personality, and so on.

A couple of years before my husband died, when I had no personal interest in the information, my dental hygienist diverted my attention from her probing by fascinating me with her story of meeting her husband through the "VNP Club" (not its real name), a matchmaking organization for Jewish singles. VNP advertised regularly in my local newspaper so, now single, I called the number, received a package of information through the mail, completed the application form, and sent it in. After several weeks of not hearing from VNP, I called. The proprietor didn't remember my application but said she would be happy to meet me.

"I thought you considered me a hopeless case," I laughed.

"There are no hopeless cases," she insisted. "There's someone for everyone."

We arranged to meet at her office the following Tuesday at eleven in the morning.

Carefully dressed, I set off for the meeting feeling embarrassed, silly, and very much aware of my years and the strange circumstances. I arrived a bit early and found the door to the VNP office locked. After a cup of coffee in a nearby cafe, I went back at exactly eleven o'clock. The door was still locked. I waited. And waited. At noon, I pushed a note under the door and went home. Investigating a dating service was weird enough at my age. Being stood up by the matchmaker was surely an indignity of high order.

Follow-up calls to the VNP office were never returned; no explanation was ever given. I could have assumed that this agency *did* deem my case hopeless, but more likely, I decided, this was simply a poorly run, understaffed, and disorganized operation, and I must try others for a truer picture of the matchmaking business.

Undeterred by my experience, I contacted several other matchmakers to learn what they offered. The most expensive service I came across was, according to its videos, "the Rolls Royce of matchmakers." This service included a psychological evaluation, with a Rorschach test, as part of the preparation for making a match. Other advance work included a handwriting analysis, an evaluation of financial holdings, a private investigator's search to discover any criminal or prison record, a medical examination complete with a test for HIV/AIDS, and a horoscope based on date and time of birth! The clients also received several hours of one-on-one consultation with the matchmaker so that she could get a clear picture of each client's requirements.

"I give them what they need, not what they want—and they forget what they want," said the proprietor of this establishment, who claimed to have matched 6,000 couples in some twenty years of business.

In her waiting room, prior to interviewing the matchmaker, I spoke with one of the clients, a woman in her upper fifties.

"How long have you been with the service?" I asked.

"Just over two years."

"And have you been pleased?"

"Well, not really . . . but that may be my fault. I've had some problems and I haven't been as interested in the search as I might have been."

"How much did the service cost you?" I asked, very nosey—but that's my job!

She hesitated before telling me: "Thirty thousand dollars."

I hope I managed to maintain my professional demeanor and that my jaw didn't drop too noticeably.

"What made you come to this agency?" I asked.

"Well, I kept seeing ads in the paper and when I called, they invited me to a seminar. She [the proprietor] is very persuasive, so I signed up."

I, too, had been invited to one of these seminars when I first called the office for information about the service. About 150 people paid the ten-dollar fee, which was waived for me as a guest of the agency. The ten dollars bought delicious light refreshments and a motivational talk, given by the matchmaker herself, who made a dramatic entrance to wild applause after an impressively choreographed introduction by her elegant, beautifully dressed staff.

"I haven't time to provide my service for everyone who would benefit from it, so I am going to *give* you my secrets for finding a good match!" She presented us all with a book filled with her "secrets" on how to find "marriage material." These were largely sensible ways to build self-esteem—essential if a person is to talk comfortably and with confidence to strangers.

In reality, these "seminars" *were* a way to recruit new clients. Two days later, a telephone call invited me to a personal consultation with the matchmaker, my name and phone number having been taken from the application form filled out when I attended the seminar.

A long interview with a staff member at the matchmaker's office made clear the kinds of people who would pay $30,000 and more—*much more*—to have someone find them a spouse. (If you are the least bit cynical, you are probably saying something like, "That kind of person must be not too bright—and have more money than sense!")

"Our clients are all well-established, 'together,' accomplished achievers who have everything—full lives—except someone to share it all with, and no time to do the kind of exploration you are doing for your book," the counselor told me. "They want someone to do that for them—and are willing to pay that someone to cut through the weeks and months of finding out about a man or a woman's background."

Despite the very high prices she charged, this matchmaker gave no guarantees, claiming to find partners for about 60 percent of her clients. She was always looking for matches, she said, even in her leisure time.

"I'll approach a man in a restaurant if he looks likely for one of my clients. I went over to someone the other evening and asked him outright if he was married! 'It's not your business!' he said. 'That's where you're wrong,' I told him. 'It *is* my business.' "

Interestingly, this very high-priced matchmaker closed up shop and left our town not long after our meeting, under something of a cloud. Whether her clients ever got back any part of their paid-up-front fees is unknown. Perhaps they should have hired a private detective to investigate *her* before they invested their money in her service!

Because matchmakers are now so visible a part of the singles scene and recruit so aggressively, I examined several more before choosing two to investigate from the inside as a "client." At each of the agencies, I gleaned some fairly obvious snippets of dating wisdom from the resident psychologists and proprietors. For example:

- "Lots of people have had bad experiences with members of the opposite sex. I tell them one bad meal doesn't mean all meals are going to be bad."

- "People are not always ready for a new partner, still hung up on some old, unhealthy relationship. They say there are no good men (or women) out there and dating is boring. When they are ready, they find attractive people everywhere."

Most of the matchmakers that I dealt with operated out of luxury suites in high-rent commercial districts—Beverly Hills and Century City in Los Angeles, for instance. This fact alone makes high overhead unavoidable, and contributes to the cost being paid by the customer. The majority of these agencies provide clients with a set number of "matches" for an agreed-upon number of years, with some offering "lifetime" services. Few make any concrete promises.

One company owner boasts that he provides a "psychological director" to interview and test all clients, asserting that this makes his agency better able to determine who is *not* for you rather than who *is*. Despite charging several thousand dollars for his services, he was unable to provide any statistics concerning his agency's success rate, as he had not been in business long enough to create a sufficient database. I was directed to his office by "Bill," one of my male interviewees who had been recruited by this particular service after placing a personal ad in an upscale city magazine. He was not charged a fee. However, he had to agree to a medical test at his own cost, as well as psychological testing. He is now "on call" as a possible match for female clients interested in a healthy, educated man over seventy years of age.

Don't Pay Too Much

I did discover, too late for the health of my own pocketbook, that fees can sometimes be negotiated, and that some agencies waive their fees entirely for "desirable" clients such as Bill. In addition, I found out that free "memberships" are sometimes given away as prizes at recruiting seminars.

One matchmaker told me that his agency has no set fee. After the initial consultation, his staff sets a fee based on its perception of how difficult—or easy—the client will be to match. His fee for a guaranteed number of matched introductions ranged from $3,000 to upwards of $20,000.

Without exception, the staff at these agencies fawns over prospective clients—at least, until they've signed them up. Well coached in the art of flattery, they all complimented my hair, my eyes, my charm, my clothes, and anything else remotely connected to my being. On one occasion, this barrage of adulation even spilled over into the elevator. While on my way up to a matchmaker's office, two staff members who had entered the elevator with me correctly guessed where I was headed. One said to the other, just loud enough for me to hear, "Oh, what a *lovely* lady that is!" This could be heady stuff if you fail to recognize it for what it is—an intrinsic part of the sales pitch.

A Tale of Two Matchmakers

As part of my investigation, I took on the role of "paying customer" and decided to enlist the services of two agencies. One was in the medium-to-high-price range. The other charged fees so relatively low that I wondered how it could stay in business. As it happens, it didn't!

The more expensive service—we'll call it "Barbara Baker's Individual Search"—claimed that I would be provided with six potential matches in a two-year span. If fewer than the stated six were delivered, a prorated amount of the fee would be refunded—unless I found success through their matchmaking efforts prior to using the allotted six matches. The cheapie service—we'll call it "Ladies First"—did not give me a minimum number of matches, but claimed that it would search for suitable partners for six months.

The Royal Treatment

Why would a person with an average middle-class income lay out thousands of dollars, upfront, for the mere chance to meet "Mr. or Ms. Right"—or even "Mr. or Ms. Not-Too-Wrong"? Just how did Barbara Baker go about presenting her agency as deserving of such a sizable financial investment?

First, her advertisements invited you to an on-site inspection of her agency. "Drop by the office for coffee and a chat. Come several times. *No obligation.*"

Upon my arrival, I was warmly greeted by a smiling office receptionist. Then, Barbara Baker *herself* took time from her busy schedule to have a "getting to know you" chat with me. This conversation proved to be rather one-sided, devoted almost exclusively to Ms. Baker's enormous success and to the virtual "Singles Empire" she had founded. She boasted of having thousands of singles on her mailing lists, and of having promoted legendary parties and "mixers" all over the county.

"I don't recommend the parties for you," she insisted. "The men are too unsophisticated for a lady of your intellect—and," she added, peering into my face, "you deserve the best. You are a very pretty woman." I smiled inwardly at both her transparent flattery and the blatant puffery of her sales pitch. I was well aware that the fees paid by partygoers generated very little profit as compared with the full-blown individual searches. And I was just as aware that Ms. Baker thought she might have a "live one" here who might sign up for the entire works.

I was then assigned to "Janice," one of the agency's "program directors," who would answer all my questions.

"I've heard that to meet contractual obligations," I said disingenuously, "some agencies use their own family members to make up the number of 'matches.' How do I know you won't do that here?"

Janice appeared shocked at the very notion. "We have no need," she assured me, "We have so many wonderfully eligible men in your age group. Wait just a moment," she called over her shoulder as she ran out of the room. She soon returned with a sheaf of files, and dropped the stack on her desk with a thud. "These are just the *tip of the iceberg*. Most of the men are currently being 'matched,' so their files aren't available. These are just a few for you to look at so you can see the caliber of men who sign up for our service."

She allowed me to look at several photographs of men in their fifties and sixties, and gave me "vital information" about their requirements and their incomes. Not one of them earned less than "a hundred thou a year," she made sure to add.

"Do the men pay the same as the women?"

"Absolutely," she replied. "Our men are serious about finding a life partner and are willing to pay. We have such a good reputation! We have successfully matched hundreds of couples. We are always thrilled when our clients marry."

I was still not persuaded to hand over my money—remember, full fee to be paid in advance—so Janice encouraged me to think about it further before signing. She told me that I should complete a short "profile" before I left the office so she could begin finding a suitable match; the longer, more detailed questionnaire would be answered at home.

"I've already got two or three wonderful men in mind for you," she said temptingly.

At our next meeting, Janice explained that the first introduction would be made within thirty days. After two months, another introduction would be arranged, and I could even date *both* men if I wished.

After another two months, yet another man would be provided—unless I told the agency to "Hold it!"

Services Rendered

A week or so later, for the high purposes of research, I bit the bullet, paid the fee, and prepared to write my report. Shock of shocks, Janice abandoned me as soon as the check was snatched out of my hand. I was shunted over to "Fran," and I never saw or spoke to Janice again. I suppose that her job was done.

Fran, who was in her twenties, held the official title of "matchmaker." She told me that she, in conjunction with Barbara Baker, would use my detailed profile to find at least six suitable "gentlemen" over the course of the contract. At least, that's what she said.

The profile—a list of personal characteristics and preferences—was drawn from a series of questions I had answered in detail. These questions concerned my tastes in music and the arts; the different activities I enjoyed and expected to share with another person. Did I like travel? Sports? What did I like to read? A number of questions concerned my temperament. Was I an extrovert or an introvert? Did I plan ahead or was I more spontaneous? Was I romantic? Religious? What was my preferred age range and level of education?

I had already discussed at length with Janice the kind of mate I was looking for, and I assumed that this information had been passed on to Fran. It had not. But in my case, it made no difference. Fran, it seemed, was not going to be my matchmaker for long. She was coming down with the flu, or so she thought. She was getting married in less than a month and had important personal matters on her mind. Further, she'd only had experience matching younger people, and was not comfortable matching people in my age group.

Despite Fran's obvious indifference to my own concerns, I tried to be patient, especially since I had now paid my money! I wanted to know where Fran had met her husband-to-be. Did she find him through the agency? No. She'd placed a personal advertisement in a local magazine targeting her ethnic group. *Hmm.*

I was soon passed along to "Brenda," yet another "matchmaker" who, in consultation with Barbara Baker, studied the files to find me my first match. They finally came up with "Irving." Brenda informed me that although he had no college education, he was the right religion, tall and nice-looking, and most importantly, "warm and caring"—characteristics that I soon learned were used to describe every potential match.

Irving took some tracking down. Since his second divorce, he'd been living with his daughter in another county. After days spent trying to contact the elusive Irving, Brenda decided he wasn't of "high enough quality" for me, and that she would look for someone else.

More than a week later, Brenda found "Cliff" in her files. "Cliff" was another twice-divorced man, an artisan who had his own business. He was, of course, "warm and caring," hard-working, and serious about marriage. Coincidentally, he, too, could not be contacted. I was told to be patient. He might be out of town. After another week, Brenda discovered that "Cliff" was "in a serious relationship"—but not with someone from Barbara Baker's Individual Search.

Brenda was still trying to find me a first "match," but she was getting noticeably more desperate as she combed through the files. She then suggested "Carl," a salesman who'd been married for fourteen years, but divorced for the last quarter century. "Why would I be interested in this man?" I asked. I wondered what had happened to the rest of that "iceberg," the tip of which had yielded so many interesting and successful men. Brenda had no answer. Further, she had no file on Carl. "It's someone Barbara knows," she informed me. *Aha!* Perhaps the rumor that matchmakers called their own brothers-in-law to fill the breach was not entirely untrue.

I did meet "Carl," who proved to be a decidedly ill-matched "match," nothing at all like his profile. I called Brenda to complain. "Do you realize that lunch with that man cost me a whole bunch? (One sixth of the agency fee.) It wasn't worth it!"

Brenda suggested I visit the office for a more intensive discussion of what I was looking for. But I was told that I was being handed over to "Kay," yet another "matchmaker." The agency staff was in a constant state of changeover.

Kay—and the omnipresent Barbara Baker—pored over some more files and discussed them with me. To my surprise, one of them was for "Rick," the man I had met months before through my own personal ad in *The Nation*; the same Rick who'd been indignant that I was doing research for a book, and who had been so willing to let me pay for my own lunch. I couldn't imagine that he would fork over thousands of dollars for *this* kind of service.

"I've already met him," I told Kay. "So don't bother with that one."

By coincidence, Rick called me a few days later, and he described his own experience with the Barbara Baker agency. Rick said the introductions he had received so far had not been interesting, and the women were no more well-matched than those he'd met through the personals at a fraction of the cost. He had indeed paid well for the services, even though he had negotiated the fee down to about half the asking price. I thought it kind not to tell him that had he been more persistent, he need not have paid at all!

Caveat Emptor!

Six "matches" were eventually dredged up for me by Barbara Baker's agency over the course of a year. All were described to me in absolutely ecstatic terms. "Just right for you!" "This is the one for you. I feel it in my bones!" All were ill-matched, and some were wildly, even *hilariously,* unsuitable! Religious beliefs, politics, interests—we had hardly anything in common, except our growing mutual fury with the Baker agency.

One of the men—a psychiatrist who sounded as if he might actually be interesting—informed me on our first and only meeting that he regularly consulted a psychic so he could see into his future. Another took great pleasure singing in karaoke bars and gambling in Las Vegas. These pursuits were not of the slightest interest to me, as my detailed profile should have readily indicated. Yet another was a generous and rich man, who spent all of his leisure hours buying presents for his friends and family. He just loved to shop! I, on the other hand, *hate* shopping—*and Kay knew this.* If I should go to Hell when I die, I am certain that I will find myself trapped in one of those giant malls for all eternity!

The men with whom I had been "matched" were as bewildered and befuddled as I was. We kept asking each other, "Did they even look at our profiles? What do they mean by 'matching'?" I cannot help but suspect that "matching" meant that *any* male who was available was suggested by the agency, so they could provide the requisite number of matches stipulated by my contract without doing an iota of actual work. Each person I agreed to meet was counted against me, however unsuitable he turned out to be.

I hope that my experience with Barbara Baker's agency gives you pause, and I encourage you to consider carefully before investing any amount of money—let alone thousands of dollars—for the "privilege" of meeting a set number of "matches." It's quite possible that this particular organization has brought some couples together who have ultimately gotten married. But I have calculated that their overall success rate is poor. Look at the agency's own advertisements. Barbara Baker claims in her ads that she has over 60,000 members in her "singles organization," and that she has histories and detailed background information on 3,500 professional men and women. One of the ads lists the number of actual marriages as "more than 224"; yet a figure of between 300 and 400 is presented in earlier advertisements. Further, it is unclear which membership "pool" these marriages were derived from.

You should also be concerned about the manner in which male clients, particularly older men, are recruited. Based on my own experience with Barbara Baker's agency, and my research of many other such companies, it is a certainty that a number of men are recruited for the sole purpose of boosting "eligible partner" file numbers. These men operate under "private arrangements," meaning that they don't pay for the service. One man told me he was a "personal friend" of Barbara Baker; another was her accountant; a third told me that he served as "inventory" for this and other agencies.

Kay responded with indignation when I told her that one of her matches considered himself "inventory." "I work hard to make *genuine* matches between serious people who are marriage minded. Tell me which man said that to you—and we won't use him any more!"

I liked Kay, and I wanted to believe that her response was genuine. But my reservations about expensive matchmaking services remain unchanged. In fact, my doubts were bolstered after a recent discussion I had with "Millicent," one of the interviewees who shared her online dating experiences with me for Chapter 3.

Millicent was registered with a "matchmaker"—not Barbara Baker's agency, but another company with a similar operation. "I discovered they have really limited resources," she told me, "although they are terrific salespeople." This agency introduced Millicent to men who were almost laughably unsuitable. "One wouldn't imagine any 'matching' had been done at all," she told me. "It was hideously expensive but I thought I would be spared the time-consuming sifting through and sorting out. Not so."

Unexpected Complications

I have even less to say about "Ladies First," the low-end matchmaking service I subscribed to for research purposes. Ladies First was described by its proprietors, "Philip" and "Mary," as "a matchmaking/dating service." Philip and Mary told me that they had organized dating events such as "singles mixers"—dances and parties—before forming their new agency.

To keep costs low, Ladies First operated from Philip's oceanside apartment. The living room had been converted into an efficient, comfortable office, equipped with computers, filing cabinets, and telephones. A glorious view of the Pacific filled the huge picture window.

The initial fee, designed to encourage enrollment, was $150 for a six-month membership, with a guaranteed full refund if a client changed her mind about joining within one month of signing.

"How can you afford to charge so little?" I wanted to know.

"Only by keeping overhead low and volume high. Neither of us draws a salary yet."

Unlike Barbara Baker, Philip and Mary were told from the start that I was researching the singles scene for a book, and were eager to answer questions about their enterprise.

"To serve our women clients," they told me, "we have a pool, so far, of over one thousand men." It was from the *men* that they derived most of their revenue. Unlike female clients, men did not pay for membership, but were charged a fee for each individual introduction. Both the men and the women regularly received a mailer of available matches containing computerized photographs and brief printed descriptions.

Mary promised she would "check over everyone who comes in with you in mind, and I'll call you as soon as I find someone suitable." She added, "We'll look for someone really special for you." She raved about my talents and "class" and looks. "You remind me of Deborah Kerr—such a lady! You deserve the best."

Inexplicably, several weeks passed without any word from Ladies First. I telephoned the office and was told by Philip that because I was Mary's client, I should call her at her home. When I called Mary, she informed me that the organization was "re-forming." She and Philip had had a slight difference of opinion—to say the least. She was charging Philip with assault with a deadly weapon! He had actually tried to run down a friend of hers with his car. This incident was the culmination of a series of "disagreements" between the partners about how much time each was investing in the service, and whose concept for business operations was the right one.

Philip was continuing to operate Ladies First as a dating service, but without the matchmaking component. Mary, who found herself shut out of Philip's apartment, could not access her files, and therefore could not serve her clients. As far as I know, the partners' dispute remains unresolved.

The old saying "You gets for what yer pays" did not apply to the matchmakers with whom I dealt. It didn't matter whether the agency operated out of luxurious settings or makeshift quarters. In truth, I got *nothing* for my money. The best advice I can offer is that you should investigate carefully, consider as many different options as possible, and, as with any business transaction, read every letter of the fine print before signing a contract.

Before Signing With a Matchmaker . . .

If you decide to try a matchmaking service, a number of points should be kept in mind if you are to avoid problems, frustration, and disappointment. Here are some proven methods of checking the quality and reliability of these services:

- Visit at least three agencies to compare costs and services.

- Check with the Better Business Bureau or your state licensing board (or both) to ascertain whether an agency has any past or pending legal actions against it.

- Ask to be referred to satisfied clients. The agency might respond that their clients are rarely willing to disclose that they met their spouses via this method. You should respond that a truly "satisfied" customer would be more than happy to discuss her experience. Be persistent.

- Ask how long the agency has been in business, and beware of "fly-by-night" entities.

- Learn how many marriages have resulted from the agency's efforts during the preceding two years. Make specific reference to your own age group.

- Ask how many men in your age range they have on their register.

- Ask how they recruit their male clients.

- Ask how they investigate their male clients.

- Get an exact figure of the cost for the agency's services, and a definitive description of what "services" are included.

- Ask about methods of payment. Does the agency require their full fee in advance, or can you pay in installments?

By doing a little detective work, you will be able to separate fact from fiction in matchmaking services.

DANCES AND SOCIALS

Many people prefer to go to dances and socials rather than using matchmaking services. These events present an immediate opportunity to meet several different potential partners, and to determine for yourself if any of them are likely matches. Two women that I interviewed during the course of my work, one age sixty-four and one age sixty-seven, met their current husbands at dances for fifty-plus singles.

In most towns across the Unites States, churches, temples, and senior centers offer dances and mixers for senior singles. Dances for the fifty-plus set are often held during the afternoon on weekends, so there is no need to worry about being out alone after dark. The bands are often very good, playing the music of the 1940s and 1950s, as well as more contemporary dance tunes. Church and temple dances tend to be relatively inexpensive—a few dollars for members, a couple of dollars more for visitors. Singles dances organized by private entrepreneurs are usually a bit more pricey. Tickets are usually available at the door, and refreshments are often provided at reasonable prices. Call your local church or temple for information, and watch your newspaper's guide to weekend activities for details.

Although most advisors suggest that singles go to dances and other similar functions on their own, I have found that men are not always reluctant to approach women in groups. I went to a dance by myself, but soon began talking with the women at my table. This did not appear to deter the men, and each of us had many dance partners during the evening.

Nowadays, it is no longer considered gauche for a woman to ask a man to dance with her; in fact, many dance sets are designated as "Ladies' Choice." You may have to summon up your courage if you are shy, but rest assured that approaching a prospective dance partner gets easier with practice. Many men have told me that *they* often find it difficult to approach a woman for a dance, as not all women are socially tactful. One man's request for a turn around the floor was dismissed with "You're not my type!" The man retorted, "I'm asking for a dance, not to *marry* you!"

Once you're out on the dance floor with a partner, you'll have the chance to learn a little bit about him—and to smile your most fetching smile, if that's how he makes you feel!

OTHER SINGLES EVENTS

The needs of single people are being catered to more and more by various organizations. Conversation evenings and other events are held in most communities, and many are heavily advertised in the local media.

While the majority of these events are aimed at younger people, some organizations, such as Parents Without Partners, welcome people of any age. So even if your children are grown up, you are still eligible. Other events are arranged specifically for the over-forty and over-fifty singles.

Many local newspapers publish a calendar of singles events on a specific day of the week. Some events I have seen listed recently include:

- "The Tennis Players: Meet, Play, Travel, 40 plus."

- "Singles Parties, 15 men, 15 women. Different parties for different age groups. Dinner. Dancing aboard boat."

- "A night on Broadway: Show tunes party with singers. Sing-along . . ."

- "The Big Difference. Party for Big Beautiful People."

- "Golf Fore Singles: Men and women. Dinner after."

- "Singles Walk. All ages."

- "Gourmet Dining Adventures for Singles."

- "Good Conversation and Delicious Dessert. 40 plus."

Church and temple newsletters also list a variety of singles' events for all age groups. Even if you haven't attended religious services for years, make a call. Not only will you be welcomed, but you may also find yourself recruited to help organize a future party, dance, or concert.

I attended a number of singles conversation evenings, some for mixed ages and some for the fifty-plus crowd. These can be enjoyable if you find a compatible group and if the topics interest you. Usually, there's a charge of ten dollars and up, which includes refreshments and soft drinks. Conversation topics can range from financial management, to travel, to relationships with adult children.

Many of these gatherings—especially in California—are run by therapists and psychologists as an extension of their regular practice. These gatherings are as much a way for people to vent their feelings about their pain and loneliness as they are an avenue to meet members of the opposite sex. People often talk freely about their personal experiences, their hurts and disappointments, and their hopes for meeting the right person. Sometimes the conversation might feel too confessional for you. But other evenings may provide fascinating opportunities to discuss and discover different ways of living. You may make new friends—of either sex—or you may even meet a man you like enough to meet outside of the group setting.

At one gathering, the speaker dealt specifically with finding suitable partners, so I listened carefully and took notes! Much to my amusement, when I looked up from my note pad, I found that the group's members were less interested in hearing what the speaker had to say than in stealing glances at each other! During the refreshment break, there was considerable exchanging of cards and phone numbers and arranging of future dates.

Nonprofit singles groups for the fifty-plus crowd also hold conversation evenings in private homes, as well as organizing activities such as bowling leagues, museum trips, and theater outings. Travel clubs provide another way to meet members of the opposite sex. Travel agents should be able to help you find an ocean or river cruise or foreign travel plan for groups of mature singles. Look through your AARP (American Association for Retired Persons) magazines and newsletters, too, for information about travel for single people.

If you love the outdoors, you might want to get involved with the Sierra Club. This organization is concerned with preserving the environment and with conserving the natural wonders of the earth. Sierra Club Singles offers outdoor activities targeted specifically at singles in a broad range of age groups.

As you begin exploring some of these possibilities, you will discover that there are plenty of opportunities to meet other singles in your area. A few telephone calls might lead you to local umbrella organizations that publish details of every singles event for miles around. For a small membership fee, you can be placed on their regular mail or e-mail lists.

In this chapter and in the previous one, we looked at a range of *direct* ways to meet members of the opposite sex: personal advertisements in newspapers and magazines, online dating services, matchmaking services, dances and socials, and singles events. Now let's turn to other, less direct resources.

5

Enriching Your Life
While Looking for Love

*C*urrent medical research is documenting what most of us have long known—that keeping active, intellectually and socially as well as physically, is good for you. "Use it or lose it" applies to one's mental acuity and one's social skills as well as one's libido! Further, experts in gerontology make a clear distinction between passive aging and active aging. To engage in successful aging demands a conscious commitment to continuing self-education, both for its own sake and for the sake of your well-being.

Only 10 percent of Americans sixty-five and over have a chronic health problem that restricts them from major physical activity. Some of us, including those still many years from sixty-five, may need a little push to reap the benefits of getting out of the house, enriching our lives, becoming involved in some pleasurable activity—and perhaps falling in love in the process.

Even if you don't feel ready for the more direct ways of looking for love, consider the list of possible life-enriching activities that I have gathered for you here. Choose something that interests you and follow through! At the same time, let yourself approach and be open to possible new friendships.

Draw on your new-found courage and introduce yourself to that man in the group who is without a partner and who might be pleasant company. If there's a man sitting alone at a concert, or studying the same painting at the museum, smile and say hello. How can it hurt? If you are out in the world, alive and alert, there is no end of ordinary ways to bump into people, start a conversation, go for coffee and . . . This may be the stuff of stories in romance magazines, but it's also the stuff of real life. Men and women chat over the water cooler at work; their shopping carts get entangled in the supermarket; they watch their laundry going around together at the laundromat; or, as happened to me, they meet while doing their regular stint of jogging or walking.

For many years, since my late husband and I moved into the house in which I still live, I have walked the four miles around the reservoir near my home four or five times a week. As a happily married woman, I was only dimly aware of "The Lake" as a place to meet members of the opposite sex. After I was widowed, although I had seen "Terry" running with a small group of other men, I had not given him any thought. Apparently, though, he had noticed me. One day, he left his group and began to walk and talk by my side. I was pleased when, a week or so later, he invited me out to dinner.

If you never leave your house, you'll meet no one other than the person who reads the gas meter. When you are involved in something you like, you will almost certainly meet new people and make friends of both sexes. Yes, it may turn out that the man you spoke to might not be friendly—or single—but the next one might be. In the meantime, you are doing something you enjoy.

The world is rich with marvelous opportunities for realizing your talents, for expanding your horizons, for making new friends. This is *your* time.

CHURCHES, TEMPLES, AND OTHER RELIGIOUS AND SPIRITUAL ORGANIZATIONS

Churches and temples offer a wide range of social and socially conscious activities that may provide outlets for your "giving" side. But hardly any "giving" is entirely altruistic. "Give and you shall receive."

Within one week, a church and a temple in my neighborhood put on a Civil War Band Concert; a comedy night, the proceeds going to a food bank; a hilarious set of "readings"—some by professional standup comedians—of the biblical story of Esther; a pot-luck supper for singles; and a bridge night. You may find congeniality and a sense of community at the church or temple you were associated with as a child, or, if you feel more spiritual than religious, you may be more comfortable with the Unitarians or another liberal, noncreedal church. The "Religious Directory" in the Saturday issue of my city's newspaper lists sixty-two denominations with more than three hundred places of worship or spiritual awareness!

If you are already a churchgoer, you know that many churches provide all kinds of services to the community. You may find a cause that appeals to your philosophy and that satisfies a personal need to be of service while being among like-minded people. This need not be the more obvious kind of "doing good," but may involve putting on orchestral or choral concerts, organizing festivals, or helping with celebrations. People are always needed to advertise, to sell tickets, and to raise money. You will be welcomed if you bring any of these skills, or even if you just bring your willing self. You can be sure they'll find something for you to do!

Churches and temples also offer courses and group discussions that you might enjoy on topics both religious and secular. If you would like to have some influence on the future direction of your church, you might consider serving as an active board member or on a committee that will debate an issue that is of concern to you.

MUSEUMS

Most cities boast at least one museum; large cities offer several. As a member of the Los Angeles County Museum of Art, I have firsthand knowledge of the many activities and specific programs that may be offered by a museum near you.

Museums do not just house their own permanent holdings of paintings and other works. They also host visiting exhibits from the world's finest collections. Over time, my museum has offered splendid guided tours of a "Sargent in Italy" art exhibit, an "Ansel Adams" photograph exhibit, and a collection of previously "hidden" paintings by the French Impressionist Caillebotte, as well as other special showings of photographs, glass, and china.

Even if you are knowledgeable about art and are already enjoying your local museum's offerings, why not look around for galleries that specialize in modern art, miniature art, antique dolls, classic cars, or some other form of art that might be new to you? I am constantly astonished by the range of museums in many American cities: museums of natural history; Jewish museums; Japanese museums; museums focusing on movies, radio, and television; aeronautic museums; and children's museums, to name just a few. The list varies from city to city, so scan your newspaper's listings of museums or check your local *Yellow Pages* to learn what is available in your area.

In addition to exhibits, many museums offer other events of interest, including:

- Silent movie programs

- Modern film classics programs

- Jazz and classical concerts, including outdoor summer concerts

- Lecture series and talks on art and art history

- Hands-on art classes

- Access to research libraries

- Occasional exhibit previews for members

If art is one of your passions, you may consider becoming a volunteer or docent (guide). This will take a little time—first for training and then for leading tours—but you will learn more about art than you could have imagined, meet hundreds of people, and make friends who have interests similar to your own. Recently, my city's Museum of Contemporary Art advertised in the local newspaper for volunteers: "No special skills are needed, only an interest in contemporary art and the desire to learn more about the artists who shape contemporary culture. Volunteers help staff the information desk, aid museum staff at special events, and provide general office and project assistance . . ." The museum in your town may have just such a place for you, or you might offer to become a "friend" of the museum before substantially committing yourself to it.

Other cultural institutions include zoological gardens, botanical gardens, and aquariums. They, too, may hold classes and offer opportunities to participate more directly than simply as a ticket-holding visitor. Again, let your local newspaper and the *Yellow Pages* guide you to activities that interest you or that might broaden your horizons.

MUSIC AND THEATER

Many of us are music or theater lovers—true supporters of the arts, even though we may not play an instrument, act, or sing. Nowadays, we can listen to the world's greatest composers on cassette or CD, and see the finest dramas on television or by renting videotapes or DVDs. These feed our soul, and can be enjoyed alone. But consider becoming *personally* involved in music-making or theatrical production, not necessarily as an artist, but in a supporting role. The community theater in your area may be struggling to stay alive. It depends on people like you to volunteer for some of the administrative and practical tasks that help keep the doors open. All small theaters have to raise money. Can you help with the intermission buffet? Can you show people to their seats? Can you help design costumes, build scenery, set up lighting or props, put up posters, man (or woman) the box office, place advertisements in local businesses? Not only will you be helping the theater, you will find yourself among actors and stage people, and will have the opportunity to talk about theater, watch rehearsals, go out for coffee with the cast and crew—in short, *enjoy* yourself!

Large city orchestras also rely on their "friends"—volunteers who love music —to run fundraising events, encourage new subscribers, produce newsletters, sell souvenirs, and more. The chamber orchestra in my town has an outreach program that presents several short concerts each year for students in elementary schools. To help the students better appreciate the music, the orchestra sends docents into classrooms to talk about the music the young people will be hearing. The docents may not be musicians, or even know how to read music, but are given a training seminar, as well as some tapes to use as teaching tools. Of course, docents attend the school concerts, and may be invited to brunches, dinners, and the concerts themselves. If this sounds appealing, make a few phone calls and see how you might fit into such a group of interested and interesting supporters or backstage teams.

Most large organizations are dependent on community support and treat their volunteers with a great deal of respect. They often sponsor award luncheons, banquets, and other activities that encourage their volunteers to continue participating and serving. Participants are made to feel that they are a valuable part of a caring family. Smaller groups also cherish their volunteers and acknowledge their contributions. You can be part of that.

If you do sing or play a musical instrument—or if you used to, but haven't sung or played a note in a long time—this may be the time to get back into it. Brush up on your skills and join a band, orchestra, glee club, or choir. Your local community college or university music department may have a place for you. You may not be playing Carnegie Hall any time soon, but you'll be having fun.

POLITICAL ORGANIZATIONS

Politics touches all our lives. It is about power at every level. It has to do not only with who wins the next election, but also with the price of bread, how often the streets are swept, and what services are provided for children before and after school.

If you want to get involved in the decisions made in your community or in the nation—decisions about social security or about civil rights, decisions about local schools or about amending the Constitution—go to it! You may wish to work with the party of your choice, or you may prefer nonpartisan politics or "grass-roots" activism.

Only you know the issues that excite you or make you angry. Read your local newspapers, including the "underground" sheets or the "free" presses, for community concerns. Follow up with telephone calls, either directly to the newspaper or to the reporter involved in the issue. Find out where the matter is being discussed, what is being planned, who is leading the "campaign," and how you might play a part.

More conventionally, you may wish to telephone the local office of your representative in Congress, in the Senate, or in your state legislature. Call your city council or the county board of supervisors. Find out what is going on so that you can make informed decisions.

People involved in politics are passionate. They'll welcome your participation, draw you into the fold, and—if you want—fill your free time with meaningful activity.

OTHER OPPORTUNITIES TO VOLUNTEER

Many of the nonprofit "helping" organizations, such as The American Red Cross, the American Cancer Society, Catholic Charities, and the Salvation Army, would not be able to provide services to those in need without dedicated volunteers. The teams of trained people dispatched by the Red Cross after a fire or an earthquake are volunteers. The people who offer information and advice at health fairs are volunteers. The men and women who research, write, and publish the organizations' newsletters are volunteers. The people who go out into the community to talk to groups about what to do before, during, and after a disaster are also volunteers.

In many city newspapers, an "Involvement Opportunities" column may point you towards other ways of volunteering your time that will both interest you and bring you in touch with like-minded people. Your help may be needed at the local animal shelter or at the hospital, for instance. Another route is to find your nearest chapter of Volunteers of America, United Way, or a similar umbrella organization. A properly placed telephone call will inform you of numerous helping organizations that need volunteers. You can learn about additional opportunities by logging onto numerous websites that will inform you of local groups. For the names, phone numbers, and websites of such organizations, see Useful Resources on page 169.

Senior Corps was designed specifically to tap the experience, skills, and talents of older citizens to meet community challenges. One of the programs, RSVP (the Retired and Senior Volunteer Program), engages people of age fifty-five and over in a diverse range of volunteer activities. Volunteers organize neighborhood watch programs, tutor children, renovate homes, teach English to immigrants, assist victims of natural disasters, and serve their communities in myriad other ways. (Again, see Useful Resources on page 169.)

The rewards for helping others are immeasurable. You will experience a genuine feeling of self-worth and usefulness. Further, a sense of comradeship develops among the members of these organizations, especially when they have worked together more than once as part of a team, traveled together to a disaster site, and shared some of the same experiences. This comradeship can, and often does, develop into affection. Volunteers can be of any age, but retired people often have more time to be of service than younger people. You'll find lots of active, caring "silver foxes"—men as well as women—among the ranks of volunteers.

DISCUSSION AND CONVERSATION GROUPS

Some of us love to talk! But if we live alone, we miss ordinary talk. And if we no longer go to work, we miss worldly, trade, and intellectual talk. Fortunately, a wide range of discussion and conversation groups are now available.

In recent years, the salon movement has grown. Salons, which are akin to the artists' and writers' groups of the past, are found all over the country. Salons come and go, and there may or may not be one in your neighborhood, but you can certainly start one of your own around topics you care about. My friend "Joy," who lives in a semi-rural area, recently began a salon at her home. Most salons are held in private homes, and in some cases people meet regularly at one address. Other groups rotate the meeting place from home to home each month, with the host providing refreshments.

How do you find people to attend your salon? You can advertise the event in newspapers or on bulletin boards, or you can place a notice online, taking the same precautions you would if you were seeking suitable companionship of the opposite sex. (See Chapters 2 and 6.) Many newspapers provide a "Mutual Interests" section. Screen the callers, call them back, and talk at length before giving your address to anyone. For safety's sake, let a close friend or family member know what you are doing. Better yet, have that person on hand, at least for the first meeting.

How would you organize your salon? Joy, who loves to read, first asked members to select a short passage from a book that they loved or that had been influential in their lives. They were to be prepared to read the passage aloud to the group and explain why they had chosen it. The group had to be small enough for everyone to have his or her say, and large enough for a varied sampling of tastes and points of view.

A salon leader is usually elected—perhaps a different person at each meeting—to make sure that members stay focused on the topic. During the break or after the formal discussion, the participants can enjoy some social time together. At the end of salon meetings, members are sometimes given a copy of a magazine or journal article to read and prepare to discuss at the next gathering. The article may concern some aspect of the economy, the changing relationships between the sexes, or any other subject that interests the group. At other salons, a film or documentary is shown, and members use their opinions and experience to enliven the discussion that follows. Salon topics can be as varied as the groups who participate in them.

Reading clubs are another popular form of discussion group. Each month or so, a group will meet to discuss a previously chosen book. As in a salon, a leader—who generally has performed research on the book and its author—facilitates the discussion and tries to keep the group on track as members share their opinions and insights.

If you are interested in participating in a book discussion group, you might start by paying a visit to your local library or bookstore, which might either host a group or know of one. Check out library, bookstore, and church bulletin boards, too, and look for notices of area people who are starting their own book club and searching for participants.

If you can't find a reading group to your liking, consider starting one of your own. Meetings can be held at your own home or in a restaurant—whatever makes you and the members of the group feel most comfortable. Often, the hostess, who may change every month, provides light refreshments during or after the discussion.

Be aware that many publishers now offer reading group guides that provide author interviews, biographies, and questions designed to spark conversation. Some local bookstores even offer reading group discounts to make the purchase of books more affordable. As you can see, plenty of help is available to help make your venture a success!

While we're on the subject of bookstores, it's worth noting that many of the chain bookstores, as well as some independent booksellers, are becoming social centers of a sort. People who enjoy a wide range of interests can come and browse, listen to instructive lectures, drink coffee, meet old friends, and make new friends—as well as buy a book, magazine, or newspaper. Many of the bookstores stay open well into the evening; some, until midnight.

The Internet, too, has spurred the establishment of numerous conversation groups and chat clubs. If you are computer literate and have online service, you can "meet" people in cyberspace and discuss topics as varied as politics, art, cooking, and sports. Once you've gotten to know someone onscreen, you can, of course, meet them in person. Just remember that because Internet chats are anonymous encounters, the risk of being deceived is high. Therefore, if you do decide to meet a chat room friend in person, you'll want to take all the precautions you would normally take when meeting a stranger.

HOBBIES: COLLECTING, ARTS AND CRAFTS, PAINTING, AND MORE

The next time you visit your local newsstand, library, or bookstore, note the number of magazines devoted to specialized interests. Whether you collect antique toys, make homemade wine, or love unusual teas, there's probably a magazine that focuses on that area. Why? Because so many other people share the same interest! And besides providing information about the subject, these magazines usually inform devotees about numerous clubs and meetings. Now may be a good time to follow your fancy, whatever it may be, and look into some of those gatherings.

If you love arts and crafts but haven't investigated the possibilities, a whole world of activities awaits you. People who enjoy working with their hands—throwing pots on a wheel, carving wooden wildfowl, making rugs, framing pictures, taking photographs, designing textiles or jewelry—are usually eager to share their interests. Arts and crafts fairs are held all over the country, and specialized magazines will provide you with the latest trends and calendars of upcoming events you might be able to attend. But there are many other ways to get involved in arts and crafts activities. Have you checked out the offerings at your local community college or adult education program? See what classes are lined up for next term. Have you envied the group of people on the shore, painting the old mill or sketching the boats? Ask how you can join them. Perhaps you've always felt you have some talent, but you were too busy to develop your artistic side. Now is the time to go ahead, get some guidance, and meet other budding artists.

DANCING

Dancing can be a good way to meet members of the opposite sex. But if you love dancing but feel too pressured to find a partner at social dances, there are many other opportunities to explore.

Line, folk, flamenco, and square dancing do not require couples. You can attend events alone, and still enjoy hours of exercise and fun. Your community college may offer Middle Eastern, Greek, Armenian, Polish, or Irish dance classes for beginners, as well as those with more experience. The enthusiasts who take these classes, and the instructors who teach them, know where and when these dances are held. Love to dance? Then what are you waiting for?

SPORTS, FITNESS, AND OUTDOOR ACTIVITIES

Physical activity will help keep you fit, healthy, and emotionally sound. If you haven't received that message yet, you haven't been listening! Every doctor who writes for popular magazines, talks on television, or has a practice is eager to encourage us to get out there and walk or engage in another activity—after we've made sure we're ready for it, of course. Walking, jogging, hiking, biking, and swimming help us stay in shape and are enjoyable ways of meeting people and expanding our social circle.

While the solitary athlete may receive friendly nods from passers-by, members of sports clubs have access to many club activities. These may include dances, talks, and slide or photo exhibits. Organizations such as The Sierra Club promote environmental conservation and offer walkers, climbers, skiers, and other nature lovers activities geared to all levels of expertise. You can also become involved in pending legislation that attempts to thwart speculators from building in your local mountains, or you can get involved in urging your legislature to clean your polluted lakes. If you can't find the address of your local chapter of the Sierra Club, write to their headquarters, call them, or visit their website. (See page 173 for more information.)

Have you thought about learning to play golf? It's a wonderful way to spend a few hours in the open air. Tennis, although more strenuous, is also a great way to get out of the house and meet others who enjoy the sport. Many city parks offer relatively inexpensive access to these and other sports activities.

If you want to get and stay in shape, fitness classes are everywhere. You might start by calling your local community college or browsing through adult education brochures. Senior citizen's centers also offer exercise classes. The YMCA is yet another option, and has the advantage of charging fees that are usually lower than those of commercial clubs. But if money is not an issue, by all means look into the commercial health clubs in your area, such as Bally's, Crunch, Curves, Gold's Gym, Personal Fitness, Twenty-Four Hour Fitness, and so on. Many of these clubs also offer swimming pools, hot tubs, and other facilities.

Other possible activities include walking, running, bowling in a league, swimming, backpacking, yoga, martial arts, fishing, boating, and many more, depending on your tastes, your energy level, and your financial resources. You could train for and join in one of the many walkathons for charity. These activities are often listed in the "Calendar" section of the local newspaper. You can also call the YMCA or YWCA, the senior center, or the bowling lanes, or even drop in at one of your local sporting goods shops for information and flyers that advertise upcoming events and newly formed groups. Your city recreation department will also be able to advise you of organized sports activities, as well as places in your area where you can swim or play tennis. And don't forget that for almost every sport you can think of, there is a singles organization that offers opportunities to engage in that sport with other people who are interested in finding partners. A brief Internet search ferreted out singles ski clubs, sailing clubs, tennis clubs, golf clubs, and much more. If you don't have Internet access, your local newspaper should list upcoming meetings. Or, if you prefer, contact a golf course, yacht club, or other appropriate facility, and ask them what is available in your area.

TRAVEL AND ADVENTURE

You always said that when you had more time or more money, you would travel. Most of us view "travel" in rather general terms. Perhaps Paris, London, Prague, and some of the world's other great cities come to mind. You may envision yourself in the company of some wonderful partner, dashing carefree from concert to museum to theater, "having a wonderful time"—as people always seem to say on their postcards from exotic places.

You probably never pictured yourself traveling alone—and you don't much fancy it. Where's the fun if you can't share all your new experiences with someone special?

Perhaps now you *will* find a friend willing and able to take a trip with you, and you'll have great times and build wonderful memories together. If no friend is available, though, you need not sit at home, green with envy as you listen to the stories of your globetrotting friends. You can go it alone and, indeed, you may find that traveling solo has its advantages. You can go at your own pace, fast or slow; you can eat when and where you wish; you can go to a museum or visit a cathedral; or you can just spend the day reading in the park—all without having to explain yourself.

Among my most adventurous acquaintances is "Meg," a woman in her mid-sixties who, for the past eighteen years, has been on the road to many parts of the world, particularly Southeast Asia, Alaska, and "anyplace where there are mountains." She had dreamed of climbing mountains ever since she was a child. Her parents subscribed to *National*

Geographic magazine, which she would read from cover to cover. Fascinated by the stories of Sir Edmund Hillary and other such travelers, she longed for the same kinds of adventures.

Meg has done much of her traveling alone. "I wanted to go to places where my friends didn't want to go, and I decided not to wait for someone to go with."

As a lone woman traveler, she provides both inspiration and solid practical tips for other women who may be thinking about setting off alone, but are not sure how they should go about it and whether they will enjoy it.

"On your own, you are more likely to meet new people than if you are one of a couple or of a group. People are less likely to feel they are intruding and they'll talk to you."

A successful trip depends on careful planning and preparation. "Do background checking," Meg says. "Know the culture and what you need to do to fit in. Ask yourself why you might want to go to, say, Indonesia. To study the art? To learn about crafts? What do you want to see and experience? What clothing is appropriate? Learn about the people and their lives. You'll be respected for it."

As an example of how she sets up a solo trip, Meg tells of her travels in Borneo a few years ago. She had read an article about Gunung Mulu National Park, the largest national park in Malaysia, over a million and a quarter acres. For the three-day inland journey on the water, she would have to take a variety of crafts: first high-speed boats, then longboats, then river canoes. In Borneo, the rivers are the roadways.

Once Meg knew where she wanted to go, she made her arrangements through a travel agent. Within the park, she was provided with a guide—an absolute necessity—and a porter; both were Borneo tribesmen. She was then taken to the most extensive caves in the world, the prehistoric caves that were home to the early cave dwellers. Her stay outside the park was spent in hotels and camps.

Your first trip alone doesn't have to be to the interior of Borneo! Meg has been traveling alone for a long time, one major trip each year in her vacation time from her job as an administrator for a nonprofit organization. But why shouldn't you, too, plan an exciting adventure to an exotic place? Meg says she has made friends all over the world, writes to them regularly, and often goes to stay with them and has them visit her.

If I've whetted your appetite for solo travel, you might like to investigate some of the websites or read one or more of the books listed in the resource section at the end of this book. You can learn everything you need to know before setting off on travels both within the United States and abroad. Prepare for your trip as Meg did, and you may have the time of your life.

Of course, it's very possible that although you want to travel, you prefer to have someone else take charge of the arrangements. Not everyone wants to go it alone! If so, it would make sense to explore the many tour groups available. These groups offer fuss-free vacations in places as diverse as New England and Tuscany. In many cases, you may even find that the group includes other singles with whom you can share the experience. Although you can find almost any tour through an Internet search, a good travel agent can be useful in guiding you to the best tours available in your region of interest.

Cruising solo is another great option. Another fuss-free way to travel, a good cruise offers myriad luxuries and a variety of activities while taking you to fascinating places. Moreover, so-called "senior" singles cruises are often available. Again, a good travel agent may be your best friend, as she can find those cruises that match both your pocketbook and your preferences.

Finally, if you want to combine travel with education, Elderhostel may be a great option. Elderhostel, a not-for-profit organization, offers extraordinary learning opportunities all over the world to people of age fifty-five and over. You can read the classics at an American university, study art in Rome and Florence, learn about history in Spain, cycle in Great Britain or Denmark, study Aboriginal heritage and culture in Australia, and more, all without ever taking an exam! Accommodations are offered in hotels, inns, retreats, centers, and select campuses, and fees include not only lodging, but also meals, lectures, courses, field trips, and cultural excursions.

Elderhostel also offers "Service Programs" that allow you to perform valuable work as you travel to new places and meet new people. Service programs include volunteering at Habitat for Humanity, a Christian nondenominational organization that builds low-cost housing for people who lack adequate shelter; working in museums; working for historical societies; participating in archaeology projects; saving the whales—and much more. (Again, see Useful Resources on pages 172–176 for further information.)

AARP—A "Senior" Group Well Worth Joining

Many of us do not like to think of ourselves as "seniors." But don't write off AARP (American Association for Retired Persons) just because you don't like the terminology. First, remember that AARP considers even people over fifty "seniors." Second, and perhaps more important, recognize how much AARP membership can do for you.

Membership in AARP costs only a few dollars a year, and brings with it many rewards. First, AARP offers its members access to health insurance, automobile insurance, homeowners insurance, and a variety of other services. It also provides discounts on travel, hotels and motels, car rentals, online services, computers, and much more.

AARP also gives you a voice in Washington and in your state, representing you on issues like Medicare, Social Security, and consumer safety. Moreover, over 3,200 local chapters provide driver safety courses, tax prep help, and a nationwide volunteer network.

Members of AARP receive monthly issues of *AARP The Magazine*, which offers informative, entertaining, and inspiring articles about engaging yourself in the world. Finally, the *AARP Bulletin* keeps you apprised of key issues confronted by Americans over fifty.

By logging onto the AARP website, you can become a member right away and start enjoying the benefits immediately. Or call or write AARP for more information. (See page 172 of Useful Resouces.)

CLASSES, EDUCATION, AND TEACHING

Perhaps in earlier years, you were too busy raising a family or earning a living to pursue subjects of interest to you. Now, though, you may have more time on your hands. If so, you can study almost any subject in the world! Apart from all the academic subjects, like history and philosophy, literature and psychology, music and art appreciation, you will find classes in yoga, human relationships, desktop publishing, computer applications, the stock market, money management, alternative medicine, massage, chess, plumbing, interior decorating, bread baking, and so on. And also attending every one of those classes are people like you, interested in knowing more about an intriguing topic, and perhaps as eager as you to meet new people and develop friendships. Some courses, such as automobile maintenance and repair, attract more men than women—and you need to know more about your car anyway, right?

Of course, the world of education offers more than just opportunities to learn. If you have a flair for teaching, even if you lack official teaching credentials, you may be able to share your skills—career skills, as well as those like knitting, painting, and cooking—with others. Your local adult education program may be looking for someone just like you to teach a class during afternoons or evenings.

If you want to combine teaching with public service, consider training newcomers to adapt to American culture, or working with those who cannot read or write. Teaching English as a Second Language can be both enjoyable and fulfilling, as can teaching reading to all age groups. Literacy programs are often provided through public libraries or adult education agencies. A phone call to your local library should give you a start.

ETHNIC GROUPS AND GATHERINGS

The United States was once thought to be a melting pot in which people from all over the world would forget their pasts and become simply "Americans." But someone forgot to light the fire under that pot and instead, America became a mixed salad, with distinctly separate ingredients. While not everyone approves, in recent years we have witnessed the "hyphenation of America." People refer to themselves as Polish-American, Mexican-American, African-American, Irish-American, and so on. Various ethnic groups take pride in discovering or rediscovering their roots, and plan visits back to the "old country," while remaining solidly American.

Perhaps your ethnic group—be it Irish, Russian, Jewish, or one of the many hundreds of others—makes up a substantial portion of your area's population. Through religious institutions and social groups, such neighborhoods offer wonderful opportunities to meet others who share your ethnic roots. On the other hand, your area may not have such a population to draw from. In that case, you may have to do a little work to find these meeting places, but the effort can prove rewarding. The search can begin with the telephone book, or you can opt to place a free or low-cost personal ad in the "Mutual Interests" section of the newspaper. An Internet search can also yield excellent results.

CLUBS

Earlier in this chapter, you learned about a variety of clubs, from reading groups to sports groups. But there are so many more types of clubs available!

Many groups are formed so that people can share information about a specific topic. You might, for instance, consider joining—or starting—an investment club, in which people pool both their knowledge and their money to make a variety of investments. Club meetings are generally educational, and often, each member actively participates in investment decisions. Some groups do quite well!

Yet other types of clubs center on playing games such as bridge, poker, chess, Scrabble, and the like. These are not gambling clubs; they are noncommercial, with players meeting in private homes, churches, and other places conducive to small gatherings. Occasionally, you will find advertisements in the "Mutual Interests" section of the personal pages. Also check bulletin boards in libraries, coffee houses, churches, and community centers.

Be aware that this chapter has covered just the tip of the club iceberg. Think of any interest, any hobby, and somewhere, there's probably a club devoted to it. If not, with a little work, you can find other like-minded people and establish a club that focuses on the particular pursuit of your choice.

GO FOR IT!

The opportunities for you to reach out and become involved in absorbing and enjoyable hobbies, discussions, and activities, to keep learning and growing, to do some good while you make new friends and perhaps even find love, are all around you. All you have to do is recognize and seize them. I hope this chapter has convinced you that there are many ways to make your life fuller and more interesting. If even one of these ideas leads you to a new activity, a new interest, or a new friend, you're sure to be the richer for it.

6

Taking a Chance
on Love

*W*henever I mention the kinds of personal research I have conducted for this book—advertising in magazines and newspapers, answering "personals," driving to dances or other functions alone, going out to meet a man known only through a letter or a telephone conversation, chatting to a fellow hiker on a morning walk—there's always someone who draws in his or her breath and protests. "But that's so *dangerous* !" the person says. "You never know who these people are. You are taking terrible chances!"

Many of us become so immobilized by our fear of what lurks outside our door that we refuse to go out at all, virtual prisoners of own imaginings. You will not be one of those people because you will be well prepared to look after yourself!

While we *do* live in a dangerous society, and although some of life's dangers are beyond our control, we can protect ourselves against many of them. Our first step is to identify those things that place us in jeopardy; our second, to decide what we can do to avoid or reduce those risks. If a situation appears to be beyond our control, we can then decide against hazarding it. If we can come up with a method of protecting ourselves, we can become a bit more daring. Some of the risks that confront older women who are entering or reentering the world of dating and mating include physical, financial, and emotional pitfalls.

PROTECTING YOURSELF AGAINST PHYSICAL RISKS

I'm sure you know this stuff already: You have probably said many of these things to your children, again and again. They can't be said too often, however.

First, never invite strangers to your home until they are no longer strangers! This means that you are not to give your address to anyone until you feel reasonably sure that he won't hurt you when you are alone with him, and that he won't try to break into your home when you aren't there.

When you are ready to leave a message, either when people have answered your personal advertisement or when you are answering someone else's, don't reveal your surname, and give only the name of your neighborhood—not your full address.

When you meet a man for the first time, make sure to arrange a day-time meeting in a public place with other people around. Use your own transportation, and if you've come in your own car rather than by cab, train, or bus, always make sure that you have at least a quarter tank of gas. You don't want anything to prevent you from making a quick get-away, should the need arise!

Make sure you have some cash and a credit card to handle any problems that might arise, including car trouble, and always carry a cell phone with you. It's also a good idea to tell someone you trust where you are going and the approximate time you expect to return home.

Don't be scared, be skilled! I strongly urge you to take a course in self-defense, as such training will be invaluable in any physically threatening situation, enabling you to escape to safety. Moreover, your self-assurance will show, and you will radiate such strength and confidence that no one will want to mess with you!

This kind of readiness can be compared to putting a theft-prevention device on the steering wheel of your car. We know that a skillful car thief *could* saw through the metal and drive off in your vehicle, but he is more likely to turn to an easier target. Call your local senior center, community college, high school, or YMCA for information about their self-defense courses.

If you meet someone who makes you feel uneasy, don't allow yourself to be driven by him to dinner or the theater. Take your own car! If you have *strong* doubts, don't go at all!

Finally, if your relationship progresses to the point of physical intimacy, take the measures necessary to protect yourself against sexually transmitted diseases (STDs). If you think you're immune because of your age, and that only "kids" in their twenties and thirties have to worry about this type of danger, you're wrong. Anyone who engages in sexual behavior is at risk. (For a full discussion of STDs, turn to page 126 of Chapter 7.)

Margaret's Story

"Margaret," an attractive widow in her early sixties, told me about a fellow she met for afternoon coffee at a local open-air shopping mall. The man, aware of Margaret's Scottish origins, sported a tam (cap) complete with feather, tartan trousers, a tweed jacket, and a red tie. At first, she found him amusing, but as they talked, his conversation grew more and more "suggestive."

"I've known women like you," he said. "Cool, sexually aloof. And I've had success with them. I will have success with you."

"I had heard about men who 'undress you with their eyes,'" Margaret told me, "and this man made it clear he knew exactly which buttons would remove my blouse!

Even though he insisted he would never make the first move—that would come from me, he said—I grew more and more uncomfortable. And I knew that I wouldn't risk going out with him. He telephoned a couple of times, always insisting that he would be a 'gentleman' if I would go out with him—he realized his talk had made me nervous—but I didn't change my mind."

Ed's Story

Men, as well as women, have some reservations about entering into possibly dangerous situations. "Ed" told me of his hesitation about meeting a woman who responded to his newspaper advertisement. The two spoke on the telephone at some length before the woman divulged that she lived at Big Bear Lake, a region reachable by road in winter only during the day, when the icy roads thawed. As soon as evening fell, the ice would re-form and he would have to wait until the next day before returning down the mountains.

The woman invited him to stay overnight in her spare room—*really* risky on her part, as she knew nothing about him except what he chose to tell her. She promised to cook him dinner and breakfast if he agreed to make the journey.

But what if the woman was after his body? What if he were assaulted by thieves in her house? What if it was a setup to relieve him of his wallet, or even his life? He pondered all these possibilities in advance of setting off on his adventure up the mountain—and told his adult daughter exactly where he was going and when he expected to return!

As it turned out, he had no need to fear for his safety. The problem was that the lady proved a most unlikely match. "She was a nice person but, physically, most unsuitable for me. I'd told her I'm slightly built but she gave me no indication of how large she was! She towered over me, especially as she piled her hair so high it was like a steeple atop her head. She also wore *powerful* perfume, perfume that permeated the house, competing with the strong smells of frying. And I was stuck there until the next day. I felt *so* uncomfortable, sorry I'd made the trip, sorry to be so ungrateful for her efforts to please me. If we'd been able to meet locally for coffee, we'd have known immediately we were wrong for each other and we could have ended it quickly." Another minor risk is that of wasting everyone's time!

PROTECTING YOURSELF AGAINST FINANCIAL RISKS

Not all older people are financially stable, but many widows and divorced women have accumulated substantial assets. Mortgage insurance may mean that the house is paid for free and clear, and other assets may have left a widow with money to invest. Divorce settlements agreed to in joint-property states may also result in sizable holdings or income. But even the less well-off can be victims of scams, and can be preyed upon by the unscrupulous.

Fortunately, just as you can protect yourself from physical harm, you can protect yourself from financial risks. Be alert! Do not tell too much too soon. If a suitor seems overly interested in knowing about your finances, let him know that your assets are held in trust and cannot be touched without consultation with your accountant, your children, your priest, your rabbi, or anyone else you can think of!

If your suitor continues to be curious, be suspicious. Do not be persuaded to put money in any stocks or funds without first investigating them fully. And if marriage talk is in the air, discuss prenuptial agreements. Any honest person will consider this reasonable—and will want his own assets to be protected, too.

When I asked "Karen" why she had signed up with a matchmaking service and paid the incredibly high fee of $30,000, she said it was because she was afraid of being defrauded. Two of her equally rich women friends had met and married men who later were discovered to be financially insolvent. One of the men was heavily in debt, and Karen felt that the matchmaker's investigation into her clients' finances would safeguard Karen's assets.

Be aware that you don't need a matchmaker to sleuth out a prospective partner's finances. You can hire a private detective, or you can gather information through public sources. Once you learn how to track this information down, you can do so inexpensively when compared with the many thousands of dollars charged by some matchmakers. (See page 177 of Useful Resources for books on investigating a person's history.) Keep in mind, too, that very few matchmakers claim that they will protect a client's finances. Their contracts usually contain disclaimers about any personal or financial injury sustained in the course of meeting and dating one of their "matches."

PROTECTING YOURSELF AGAINST EMOTIONAL RISKS

Many of us are alert to the possibility of physical harm, but we are rarely ready for the emotional hurt that can be sustained by people who are dating. We think that because we are grown-up, we can cope in ways that younger people cannot.

As the old saying goes, "Love makes fools of the very young—and the very old," I would argue that love can make fools of us at *any* age, and that older, more "experienced" people are not immune to folly. We should know, too, that it isn't only women who get hurt. We women can cause serious emotional pain for our male counterparts, as several men have confided.

John's Story

"John" was a virgin when he married, as was his wife, and he did not believe in sexual intercourse without the blessing of the church. He and his wife felt so strongly about this that when they learned their daughter had gone to bed with her boyfriend, they threw her out of the house!

At sixty-two, John was suddenly left a widower and, given his strong feelings about sexual behavior, he was desperate to remarry, if he could find someone suitable.

"I went to a dance and we did 'line dancing'—you know, men and women alternate in the line, and each holds the neck or shoulders of the person in front. I can't tell you how wonderful it was to feel a woman's hands on my neck. It had been so long."

He met a woman he liked a lot, but her views about sex were different from his.

"She persuaded me into bed. I actually made love to someone outside of marriage. I'd never done that in my life. I was sure she would marry me—how could she not, having gone to bed with me? But she eventually made it clear that she didn't want to marry. Not me or anyone else. I felt terrible—dirty, used. I know it's women who usually say those things, but I really felt that way, *feel* that way. I loved her, too, or thought I did. I would never have slept with her if I hadn't. I found myself crying a lot, crying for my lost innocence, in a way, crying for my wife. I miss her so much. I don't think I'll ever find someone who thinks the way I do about these things."

Harold's Story

Several of my male interviewees conveyed the same sense of betrayal at the hands of women. Another widower, "Harold"—a man in his mid-seventies—fell in love and wondered why he was never asked to his girlfriend's home. Instead, she always went to *his* house. She kept telling him what a wonderful cook she was, but he was never able to sample any of her culinary creations.

"She was about sixty-five and in wonderful shape. A really beautiful woman, plump and feminine. I called her 'comely.' I found myself thinking about her all the time. I'd wake up in the morning, or in the middle of the night, and I'd hold conversations with her as though she was there.

"I did something really out of character for me. Instead of taking her to bed in my own house, I took her to New Orleans for a romantic weekend. It was marvelous! We were like a pair of young honeymooners. I thought my 'dating' days were over—and good riddance!—and I could settle down with this lady for the rest of our lives. And then she told me she was unhappily married to someone she would never divorce.

"She was using me for diversion, for sex, for fun. . . . In *My Fair Lady*, the song asks why a woman can't be more like a man. Well, some of the women are doing to men what men used to do to women: using them and discarding them. It was all a waste of time for me—time I could have used looking for the right lady. After all, time is not on my side."

Men are not so different from women when it comes to emotional hurt, but perhaps we women are especially vulnerable.

Being Willing to Compromise

In *The Cemetery Club*, a film about three widows in their fifties and sixties, one of the ladies says, "Women our age don't fall in love. It's too
painful. Like our thin bones, our hearts are thin, too, and easily hurt and
damaged." Esther, one of the widows, played by Ellen Burstyn, does fall
in love and is hurt by a man who "can't make a commitment lasting
more than twenty minutes."

The lament that men—and women, too—"won't make a commitment" is heard among single people in all age groups. Esther finally
comes to terms with her lover's reluctance to marry and settles for a
kind of "permanent temporariness." It's clear that the man cares for her
and wants to be with her, as much as she wants to be with him, but
he is terrified of being tied down. Like many older women, and some
younger ones, Esther finds she must adjust her philosophy to suit her
circumstances.

Unrealistic expectations can cause considerable anguish. A woman
who has been secure in a long marriage takes permanence and assurance for granted. She expects to remarry if the right man comes along,
and anticipates having the same kind of life she enjoyed before she was
widowed. Unfortunately for her, the man she has chosen may have
decidedly different ideas.

"I didn't want to be his *date* or his *girlfriend*," one woman, "Martha,"
told me. "I wanted to be his "*wife*," and I wasn't prepared to settle for
less. So I told him I wouldn't see him again. It nearly broke my heart.
After years of grieving for my husband, I felt as though I was bereaved
again. I don't remember ever feeling quite so lost and unhappy."

Mature people fall crazily in love, just like younger people, and the
process of breaking up causes them just as much suffering as if they
were teenagers. Emotional suffering can even be more profound in your
later years than it is for young people. A compounding of losses in later
life can lead to a sense of hopelessness and despair, a feeling that the last
chance at happiness has been taken away.

Compromise is possible if you are willing to let go of old, outmoded
patterns and accept a different way of living. Martha did, in fact, rejoin
the man she loved. Many months of separation failed to ease her longing for him, or his for her. "I decided life is just too short. We have to take
joy where we find it and being with him, even on his terms, is a joy—far

better than being without him." She would like to convince him to marry her one day, but knowing how he feels about "being tied down," she has become more relaxed about taking each day as it comes instead of planning for a distant future.

The man in Martha's life has been honest with her, and has made his intentions clear. She knows the score and has come to accept it.

Sometimes, though, even though both parties want the relationship to work, other circumstances make any permanent union impossible. For instance, children—yours or his—may intrude in ways that make marrying or living together unwise.

Gladys's Story

"Gladys," one of the women I interviewed, seriously considered marriage to "Morgan," with whom she felt she had a great deal in common—until she met his daughter. This woman, in her early forties, still felt angry and betrayed by her parents' late-life divorce, even though it had occurred many years before. She was rude to Gladys, refused to attend any events if Gladys was to be present, and behaved like a resentful adolescent, even though Gladys had had nothing to do with her parents' divorce.

Instead of being supportive of Gladys during his daughter's screaming attacks, Morgan sided with his daughter and placed the blame on Gladys. He insisted that she was not compassionate enough, and that she didn't understand about the bond between fathers and daughters. After months of enduring Morgan's daughter's verbal abuse, Gladys decided the problem was insoluble, and reluctantly broke off her liaison with Morgan.

In other cases, resentment from adult children may stem from fears of financial loss. Some parents change their wills when a new love comes along, and their children may be worried that some wily man or woman will strip them of the inheritance they think is "rightfully" theirs. If these matters are not satisfactorily cleared up, marital plans may fail to materialize.

Knowing When to Trust

When I was growing up, I believed my father when he said, "A gentleman's word is his bond," and I still trust that statement. My father was honorable in business and in other areas of his life, as was my husband, my brother, and my sons.

I have learned to be a little more cautious since my childhood. Some of the men I met in recent years laughed out loud when I recited my father's phrase. "Words don't mean anything," one man told me, "especially in business, especially between men and women." He indicated that you could rely only on what people do, not on what they say.

Whether people are truthful or not, words do mean something! Those who hear them are affected by them and act on them. To complicate things further, people hear selectively; they hear only what they want to hear and turn a deaf ear to the rest.

A man may tell you that he loves you but that he doesn't want to make a commitment. Hear him. Listen to everything he says, and not just the part you want to hear. Yes, he may change his mind at some later date, but you can't depend on that. You may save yourself considerable anguish if you accept his words at face value.

The problem of whether you can trust someone—and *how much* you can trust someone—is not easy to solve. Real trust comes with time, and with enough experience to know whether someone really means what he says. The trick is not to be swayed by a man's charming statements or by your own longing to believe what you hear.

Dealing with Rejection

The risk of rejection is a given for all women and men who date. While rejection is painful at any age, for the older person newly returned to dating, it can be especially devastating. "If you stick your neck out, you must expect to get your head chopped off!" The fear of getting one's head chopped off is enough to keep some people at home watching television or knitting.

It helps if we avoid taking rejection too personally, and remember what one of the matchmakers told me: Only about one person in two hundred will be a compatible partner for any man or woman. Translation: "You have to kiss an awful lot of frogs before you find a prince!"

Each of us represents one of many possibilities for the person we are just meeting. Odds are against the first or second person, or even the tenth or twelfth, being our soul mate. Odds are also against our being the one in two hundred for him.

You may meet a man, have pleasant or not-so-pleasant conversation for an hour or so, and never see—never *want* to see—that person again. And he may feel the same way about you. This does not mean that you are undesirable or that you will never find someone whose tastes and interests are in tune with yours. Alternatively, you may meet someone with whom you do feel an affinity—but he won't appear interested in you, won't suggest another meeting, and will seem eager to draw your meeting to a speedy close.

It's easy to take this as personal rejection—to feel hurt and to want to retreat from the game forever. But remember that some of the men you meet may have been searching for a partner for a long time. You may be the seventy-seventh woman a man has met for coffee, and he may have learned to cut quickly through the superficialities. Or he may have received eighty responses to a personal advertisement and is merely "weeding out" the unlikely ones. He may even arrange to meet you at a given time and place, and then not appear. Being "stood up" is not pleasant, but it happens now and then.

"Edgar" shamefacedly told me of arriving at a restaurant, seeing the lady sitting on a bench, as prearranged, and quickly turning on his heels and leaving before she caught sight of him. "I felt terrible about it. It was a rotten thing to do, I know, but she was so far from my type, physically, I knew it would be a waste of time. She sounded likely on the telephone but at my time of life, I know I like a well-toned, athletic kind of woman, and she just wasn't interesting to me."

I must confess my own shame at rejecting more than one pleasant man because he was not my "type." After a long and delightful telephone conversation with "Samuel," an artist who had responded to my advertisement in *The Nation,* we arranged to meet in Chinatown for a dim sum luncheon. "My son persuaded me to answer your ad," he said. "And when I told him we were meeting, he said 'I hope she has a kind heart.'"

I polished my kind heart until it shone, but despite our enjoyable telephone conversation, I found our first meeting disappointing. Samuel was just not my type physically. He had a grungy appearance accented by long, rather sparse hair that he wore in a ponytail. I prefer men with a clean-cut, tidy appearance.

However, I enjoyed Samuel's stories about travel and work, and decided not to give up on the relationship right away. Looks don't matter, I kept telling myself; character is far more important. When he telephoned me a day or so later, I agreed to go to a movie and dinner with him. I felt I owed this good man another try. Again, I greatly enjoyed his company, and the film was good and the meal tasty—but I knew there would be no future together for us.

I should add that this man was a widower who had been happily married for many years to a woman who had adored him and found him to be lovable and attractive. Undoubtedly, someone else would feel this way about him in the future, but much as I would have liked to continue our friendship, I felt it would be unfair of me to lead him on. It would be fairer to let him down gently.

While I encourage people not to give up too quickly on a new relationship, you really need not feel guilty about refusing to see someone who clearly doesn't meet your needs. You have a reasonably good idea of what you would like in a partner, and you would be unfair to yourself and to the other person if you continued along a path that was leading nowhere.

A man who saddened me was a professor who invited me to lunch at his faculty club, even though he should have known he was opening himself up to rejection. He was a delightful telephone conversationalist, and it appeared we had a lot in common. He said he was in his early sixties, but as soon as I saw him, I knew that he was in his mid- to late-seventies.

He was semi-retired, teaching just one course a year. He had warned me that he was completely hairless, so I was not surprised at his bald head and lack of eyebrows, but he had not informed me that he could barely walk and had had unsuccessful hip surgery. I gently reminded him that my advertisement had specifically mentioned finding a hiking companion, but he summarily dismissed that need as superficial. "A person like you has a life of the mind. That's much more important than the physical!"

He was so unwilling to let me go, so eager to hold onto me for an hour or two longer, that he begged me to come to his university office so he could show me some of his book and manuscript collections. I wanted to get away, but felt it would be kind to stay a little longer. Finally, as I prepared to leave, he asked me to drive him home. He had no car, as he had made a promise to his deceased wife that he would never drive the city streets. Even if I had been interested in seeing him again, it would have meant acting as his chauffeur in a city of minimal transportation options.

Rejecting someone need not be brutal. Busy people can claim that their full work schedule has put any dating plans on hold for a while. As mentioned in an earlier chapter, another effective device in cutting off a would-be suitor is to claim the return of a long-lost love: "Someone I used to care for has come back into my life." Just realize that this ploy may be a tad transparent to anyone with dating experience, and may be recognized for what it is. "I really enjoyed meeting you. You're an interesting person but I don't think we really have much in common," will do in a pinch if you want to end a relationship before it begins.

You open yourself to rejection whenever you make the first call after an initial meeting. Women are particularly reluctant to call a man for another meeting after having coffee together. "We had this wonderful couple of hours together, so engrossed in each other we didn't see anyone else around us. The most interesting man I've met for a very long time. Then, he didn't call! What should I do? I liked him so much. He said he'd like us to go to the movies together and that he'd telephone to arrange it. And he hasn't."

If you do decide to call a man you like, be prepared for the possibility that he may not even remember who you are! Carol Burnett, speaking to a room full of students at the Actors Studio in New York, told them not to take it personally if they didn't get the part they had auditioned for. "It just means you aren't the right type." It's as simple as that. You may just not be that particular man's type—but you will be the right type for someone else. Don't take the early phases of getting to know someone too seriously!

The youngish proprietor of a matchmaking agency, herself terribly eager to marry and have children before she hit forty, told me of her concentrated effort to find the right partner. She advertised, followed advertisements, went to singles mixers, attended singles seminars, did everything she could to place herself where that elusive man might be.

"In one year, I met and went out with several hundred men! Can you imagine? *Hundreds* of men! I was meeting three or four in one day! It became my work, my life, my relaxation, my entertainment, and, finally, excruciating drudgery. It got so all the faces ran together. I couldn't remember who was who. I liked that one's looks, that one's income, that one's jokes, that one's voice, that one's politics . . . but it all became impossible. I couldn't have made a decision about any one of them if my life depended on it!"

While few of the men you meet will be "interviewing" hundreds of potential mates in a year, they are probably having coffee with several people each month. A call from you may delight a man, remind him of how much he enjoyed your company, and bring forth an invitation to the movies or to dinner. Or it might not! It's up to you to decide if you want to chance it.

Life is a risky business. You take your chances every time you step into the street or climb into a car. Facing the physical, financial, and emotional risks of dating and mating in later life—and knowing how to avoid, reduce, or eliminate them completely—will allow you to enjoy your adventures fully and confidently.

7

To Bed or Not to Bed, That Is the Question

*W*hen I was growing up in my lower-middle-class community, "nice" girls were not supposed to know anything about sex. In fact, just before my wedding, I asked my mother if there was something I should buy or do to prepare. "I mean, I don't want to get pregnant straight away."

My mother waved my question away. "*You* don't have to do anything," she said. "Let your husband take care of that."

The upshot of that advice was an unplanned pregnancy in my first week of marriage. My young bridegroom, who was as ignorant as I about sex, did not know that he had to withdraw quickly after ejaculation, so his condom slipped off and nature took its course. That pregnancy ended after a few weeks, and the two of us had time to learn about birth control.

When women in the family had babies, the unmarried girls—young women—were not even let in on the details of the deliveries, especially if the births were difficult or unusual. Voices would drop to a whisper if an unmarried girl entered the room when these things were being discussed.

To say that our society has changed regarding such matters during the last several decades is a colossal understatement. Society has transformed. The once-unmentionable is talked about openly and, at times, endlessly. Television advertisements bring the most private aspects of the female reproductive system into our living rooms. While we eat dinner or sip our evening coffee, we hear all about the advantages of "winged" sanitary napkins, "vaginal moisture that lasts for days," and perfumed feminine hygiene products—unless we choose to change the channel.

Movies were once governed by the Hays Code, which allowed the showing only of closed-mouth kisses and required screen spouses to either sleep in separate beds or, if they shared a bed, to keep one foot—the man's or the woman's—firmly on the floor. The camera left the room if lovemaking began, leaving the audience to imagine what was taking place. It was very discreet—and very romantic.

A former professor of mine once told me about his fraternity initiation back in the 1950s. One of the "endurance tests" involved the viewing of pornographic movies. He described the dismay of the naïve initiates as they watched the events on the screen and then the urgent clambering over bodies in the dark as he and a couple of other young men struggled to get out—before they threw up!

Today, the same kinds of movies are routinely available for a small fee at neighborhood video stores and on cable and satellite, and are watched—one trusts only by adults—in the living rooms of ordinary families of all social classes. Sex acts are depicted in mainstream films in sweaty detail. Condom use is demonstrated in high school, middle school, and even elementary school classrooms, with bananas substituted for penises. We are now in the post-sexual revolution era.

The sexual revolution that began in the 1960s and accompanied the civil rights, women's liberation, and gay liberation movements wiped out almost all of the sexual inhibitions—and prohibitions—with which many women grew up. Younger women, especially, demanded an end to the double standard that allowed men to have sexual experiences outside marriage, but that didn't afford that same privilege to women. Now women need not "save" themselves for marriage. They have equal rights to multiple orgasms and to sexual pleasure with multiple partners. They also have equal rights to sexually transmitted diseases.

While epidemics of genital herpes, chlamydia, and acquired immune deficiency syndrome (AIDS) have put a crimp in the sexual revolution, the box has been opened, and there's no putting the lid back on. Sexuality, sexual expression, and sexual needs are no longer subjects that are only whispered about. But this does not mean that women—or men—should throw their morals and caution to the wind.

NOT ALL WOMEN WERE EQUALLY AFFECTED BY THE SEXUAL REVOLUTION

The first of the baby boomers, those born in the mid-1940s, grew up during the years of the sexual revolution and, when young, tended to take some sexual freedom of expression for granted. However, most women born in the early 1940s and before grew up with very different expectations of how decent girls should express themselves sexually. When they were young, "nice" girls "didn't," and if they "did," they kept quiet about it!

These women, single once again, are still "nice" girls who are uncomfortable with the concept of sex outside of marriage and are not sure what today's men expect of them. A beautiful woman of sixty-five, widowed for five years, told me she is "dating" two people. Neither of these friendships is "romantic," she said.

"I would love to have a companion, although living alone has its advantages. I would like to be someone's special someone. But I just can't imagine going to bed with anyone. I just can't picture any of the men I know . . . I mean, our relationships are not sexual at all. With one of them . . . we did kinda dabble, but it was just so uncomfortable, we didn't pursue it. I don't even know if any of my men friends . . ." She indicated uncertainty about their sexual powers. "You know, sex wasn't all that important, even in my marriage. Not a big part of our lives. People didn't go on about it all the time, the way they do now."

However, another woman I interviewed who has been twice widowed and is in her late sixties has had several love affairs, both during her first widowhood and during her second. To her way of thinking, sex is the stuff of life. "I have never been without it," she said.

When I first interviewed her, she was very much in love with a man she'd met through a personal advertisement. He was talking about marriage, but she wasn't sure she wanted to make that commitment. However, she also expressed some doubts about how long she could go on attracting new partners as she grew older.

Given her willingness to be "out there," I suspect that she will continue to find lovers for as long as she wants, and that it is this attitude that will make all the difference. My doctor recently told me a lovely story about her mother. "She's always had a romantic life," she said, "and she's just getting married for the third time—for love—and she's nearly eighty."

These women's varied experiences and views tend to support the research into sexuality that claims that patterns of sexual activity continue from youth to very old age. Those who enjoyed frequent or regular sexual activity earlier in their lives continue to enjoy it—if they have a partner or partners with whom to share it—while those for whom sexual activity was of little importance, unsatisfying, or even distasteful are content to let that part of their lives fade out as they grow older, even if they are married. But even those whose sex lives were dull can be stirred to sexual excitement by a passionate and patient new lover.

WHAT IS APPROPRIATE SEXUAL BEHAVIOR?

The rules concerning sex are not necessarily clear or rigid. What you decide to do regarding sex will depend on the situation—and it isn't always easy to correctly interpret another person's feelings or expectations and then to behave appropriately. Some men may be delighted if a woman indicates a sexual interest in them. Others may be completely turned off.

Herbert's Story

"Herbert," an old acquaintance, told me of his pleasure at being invited for a home-cooked meal by a woman he had known for a couple of months. They had been to the movies and the theater together several times, and he thought of her as a good friend.

She had set an elegant table decorated with beautiful silver, gorgeous flowers, and softly glowing candles. The food was excellent, the conversation was interesting, and the music on the stereo set a relaxed and romantic mood. After the meal, the woman suggested they move to the living room, where she promptly inserted a tape into the video player—a pornographic movie!

Herbert was shocked. He was offended by the film and by the woman who took such an assertive and "coarse" lead in moving the relationship along. "I simply left," he said. "Walked out. Never saw her again, and never wanted to."

David's Story

According to most of my male interviewees, such a blatant come-on by a woman is far from the norm. "David," a widower, said he'd fully expected women to be sexually assertive. "My single men friends told me that all the women are sex-starved and are ready to go to bed at the drop of a hat. This hasn't been my experience at all. Mostly, the women seem quite content to be just friends, companions, to go out for dinner and pleasant walks. They don't seem sex-starved to me. I wish more of them were! I never know how a woman will respond to sexual overtures. It's always a delicate matter."

David was propositioned by one lady soon after they met. It was a "cute meet"—a meeting between people in unlikely but pleasant circumstances. He was waiting at the appointed time in the foreign language section of a bookstore for a woman who had responded to his personal advertisement in the local paper. He'd spoken with her on the telephone, but didn't know exactly what she looked like. A woman who seemed "likely" came through the door at the precise time of the arranged meeting.

"Are you Patricia?" he asked her.

"No, my name is Emma," she said.

"Oops! Sorry. I'm supposed to meet a woman here, and I don't know what she looks like. I thought you might be her."

The woman smiled and moved away, disappearing from view. A few moments later, she came back and said, "I'm not Patricia, but will I do?"

Although David really liked the look of this woman, he found the situation embarrassing. Patricia was due any minute. "So Emma gave me her card and said I should call her if I was interested in getting together for coffee sometime."

David did call Emma a few days later, and they soon became friends. "She told me she was willing to go to bed with me, but she set up some very rigid rules on the relationship. It was to be exclusive. I was to spend every weekend with her, and three nights out of the five week nights. Also, I was to call her every day."

"Was that acceptable?" I asked.

"No. Not at all. I'm afraid I laughed at her. I said this reminds me of Shaw's *Don Juan in Hell*. Don Juan didn't want to be cut off from half the human race, and nor did I."

Emma had not assessed the situation correctly. While exclusivity in a sexual relationship is an understandable expectation for a woman, insistence on such lover-like attention before there have been professions of affection, and before the man has expressed his own wish for exclusivity, may nip any prospects beyond friendship in the bud. Emma failed to realize that feelings of commitment must be mutual and mutually expressed.

Janet's Story

Many men I interviewed believed that after a certain number of dates, a friendship should progress to include sexual expression. Usually, it was after four or five dates. "Men our age are adults, not children," one man told me. "A relationship has to move on or end. I'm not going to pay for theater tickets and expensive meals indefinitely. I'm not courting without getting what I need."

For some women, going to bed after four or five dates, or after a few weeks, is much too soon. "When he said he wanted to go to bed with me, I was so nervous," "Janet" told me. "I'd never slept with anyone but my husband, and I didn't know what to expect. I liked him so much, but after *four weeks*? It's such an intimate thing to do so soon. I'd known my husband a year before we married, and we hadn't had sex. Poor guy! Years later, we laughed about it. He said he'd absolutely *ached*. After an evening with me, kissing and cuddling, he couldn't stand up straight, he had needed release so badly. I didn't understand then. Now I do understand. But it's hard to break lifelong habits—beliefs. I still feel he'll lose respect for me. And if this doesn't work out, how many men will I go to bed with? It would make me feel . . . dirty. It goes so much against my grain."

Now, just as in "the old days," women have every right to maintain their standards. We need not feel pressured into giving in to a man who might make us feel guilty about the "pain" we are causing or who suggests that we are behind the times sexually. A woman's need for self-respect is just as important as a man's need for the release of sexual tension.

Beatrice's Story

"Beatrice," a widow of fifty-five who had been married for thirty-four years, joined a widow's bereavement group soon after her husband's death. "The women in the group talk a lot about how they would like romance, but they aren't venturing out to find it. They stay in their own circles."

Two years into her widowhood, though, Beatrice was now having a serious love affair with a man she had known for seven months, and she was finding life "confusing." "It's so exciting to be in love with someone new, yet I'm still in love with my husband."

Her husband, fifteen years her senior, had been married before and had brought four children to their marriage. They had had two children together, and Beatrice had raised her dead sister's children, too, so the house had always been filled with young people. Her husband had been ill for seven years before his death, and during the last five years of his life, the couple had had no sex life. "I had no way of knowing that was not a normal situation."

Beatrice's relationship with her lover, "Jeff," differs from her marriage in that they concentrate both on themselves and on each other. They do not live together, but they may choose to do so when they both retire. Beatrice thoroughly enjoys the relationship, but she is not yet ready to be defined by it.

"I've never had anyone take care of me this way. Jeff is very caring. I want to nurture the relationship, keep it romantic. Jeff is a romantic—flowers, candy, gifts. I'm afraid marriage would not be romantic. *My* marriage certainly wasn't, and I'm enjoying this. I'm not ready to give it up."

Beatrice told me it had been difficult to become sexual with Jeff at the beginning of the relationship. "I didn't know if my body was attractive. I didn't know if I was aging all right. I initiated the sex. He was very much a gentleman. We went off on a romantic weekend. He's been very patient and gentle. He doesn't have the same sexual appetite that I do, but he is innovative. And he has become very much more interested in sex, he tells me, than he was earlier in his life."

When Beatrice and Jeff first slept together, it was away from home, away from the furniture, the pictures, the ornaments, and the bed she had shared with her husband. "Now I can sleep with him at home. We have talked about moving somewhere else, but we aren't ready yet."

Beatrice's experience, and that of others, raises a number of issues that concern both men and women who are looking for and finding love—and sex—in later life.

THE VULNERABILITIES OF MATURE MEN AND WOMEN

Unquestionably, many older women feel nervous and embarrassed at the prospect of baring their bodies to a new man. A widow, married for more than thirty years, never doubted her husband's acceptance of her gradual "softening," but felt that a new man might compare her to all the firm-bodied women he'd been bedding lately. Divorced women, especially those whose husbands took up with women ten to twenty years their junior, expressed the same kinds of concerns about their bodies. Self-esteem takes a dive under these circumstances, and women need all kinds of assurances that they are still perceived as attractive and sexy.

We live in a society in which women of all ages are made to doubt their attractiveness. One morning, as I was walking around Hollywood Lake, I overheard a conversation between two women, one about twenty-five and the other roughly twice her age.

"You're looking really great, Louise," the younger woman said. "Working out is doing wonders for you."

"Well, thanks, Marge. I appreciate your support," the older woman answered. "But when I look in the mirror these days, I go, 'Yechhh'!"

"Don't be so dumb!" Marge snapped back. "When *I* look in the mirror, I say 'yechhh' as well. What woman is ever satisfied with the way she looks?"

It turns out that most older men are quite realistic about the women they date, accepting and delighting in the less-than-perfect figures of their partners. In fact, several men I interviewed told me that they had made love to women who'd had a mastectomy and that this was not a problem for them. One man said it was the woman's embarrassment over her scars and her constant references to them that made him uncomfortable.

An insightful article in the magazine *Health* provides us with an anecdote about the acceptance by men of women's less-than-perfect bodies. A woman who'd had a mastectomy and reconstructive surgery found it difficult at first to enter into sexual encounters with new partners. To overcome her discomfort, she talked about her experiences publicly. She also began writing about how she felt. This helped her to adjust to her circumstances.

"I've been sleeping around," she jokes, and goes on to add that for the most part, men have been wonderful. "They are not as shallow as we may think."

Aging men have their own vulnerabilities, and like women, they need reassurance that they are desirable and can satisfy a partner's sexual needs. Much of men's sense of virility lies in their ability to perform sexually, and women need to know that older men may need an especially understanding and patient lover.

SEXUALITY AND LATER LIFE

Only recently have researchers begun to study sexuality in the older segment of society. The little that was written about it in the past was filled with gloom and doom about waning abilities and diminishing desire. Older people who continued to enjoy sexual activity were made to feel like freaks, believing their behavior was unusual and abnormal. Mature males bold enough to express an interest in a woman's body were seen as "dirty old men."

Sexuality in the elderly has not been well understood, nor has it been considered of much interest to scientists, until recently—and it isn't difficult to see why this has been so. It has been only since the late twentieth century that most of us have expected to grow old. Not too long ago, most men did not live past their sixties. There was a large gap between the life expectancies of men and women.

Now both men and women can expect to live far longer than any past generation. Most lethal infectious diseases have been virtually eliminated by childhood immunizations, and even heart disease, that killer of middle-aged men, is being brought under better control. A couple can now expect to have twenty to forty years of active life after they launch their children into society as independent adults.

This is an entirely new world, and while gerontologists—those specialists who study all aspects of aging—have been busy thinking about the needs of this group, the needs they have primarily been considering are those of an increasingly disabled population.

The very old—those in their eighties, nineties, and older (centenarians are the fastest growing of the age groups)—will certainly have to be provided with services if they are to continue living independently. However, experts are realizing that for the rest of us mature adults, sexual activity may also play an important role in our lives, depending on our physical well-being, attitude, past experience, opportunity, and understanding of our changing needs.

THE PHYSICAL SIDE OF AGING

It's obvious that not everyone ages in the same way. Just go to the beach and look at the men and women in their seventies and eighties jogging along the sand, while up on the boardwalk, others in the same age range are being pushed along in wheelchairs by their spouses or attendants.

Fortunately, most of us will live our longer lives in relatively good health. And the news is positive about people remaining sexually active well into old age. Indeed, some women really begin to enjoy making love only after menopause, when they are no longer afraid of getting pregnant, and they surprise themselves—and their mates—with their passionate abandon! According to the *Janus Report on Sexual Behavior*, one of the first important studies of this subject since the landmark work of Masters and Johnson, at no age below ninety were people *not* having sex when they were interested and had a sex partner. People in their seventies, eighties, and nineties who have sex on a regular basis report that it is as gratifying as ever. The desire and ability to have sex remains an important aspect of their lives with their partners.

What about people without partners, however? Samuel and Cynthia Janus noted that many women fifty-one to sixty-four reported that after they became widowed or divorced, they did not know how to find a sex partner when they wanted one. It seems, then, that many women either do not know how to meet appropriate partners or do not have the courage to do so.

Men and women do experience hormonal changes as they age, however, changes that may affect them both physically and psychologically. These changes, in turn, may affect their level of sexual desire whether they have partners or not.

Women, Menopause, and Post-Menopause

Ever since the baby boomers began turning fifty in the mid-1990s, interest in the process of menopause has become both vocal and public. The largest group of women ever to simultaneously experience menopause has made it the subject of keen discussion. Where in the past menopause, or "the change," was feared as a condition that made some women crazy, women are now encouraged to understand what is happening to their bodies, what signs and symptoms they can expect, and what they can do to ease the unpleasant effects of menopause.

A sharp drop in the hormone estrogen accompanies menopause and can cause dryness and shrinkage of the vaginal and peri-vaginal areas, as well as discomfort or even pain during sexual intercourse. To combat these effects, many gynecologists routinely prescribed hormonal replacement therapy (HRT), which was also thought to help strengthen the bones, which weaken as the body's production of estrogen declines.

In 2002, however, the early results of a major study of HRT conducted by *The Women's Health Initiative* (WHI) indicated very slightly raised risks of heart disease and breast cancer when HRT was used. Many women, therefore, became hesitant to use or continue this therapy. This study of HRT was halted, however, it did find slightly lowered incidences of bowel cancer and bone fracture among the subjects using HRT than among those using a placebo.

Women, in consultation with their doctors, have to weigh the odds. Many use HRT for a limited time to control the hot flashes and other unpleasant effects of menopause. Others experiment with smaller dosages, trying to lessen the risks while gaining the benefits. Still other women seek alternative treatments, such as the herb black cohosh and other "natural" remedies, none of which have been as rigorously tested as HRT.

One option to HRT in pill form is the topical application of estrogen cream intra-vaginally. Small amounts of estrogen are absorbed into the vaginal tissue, moistening the area and thickening the vaginal lining without causing the side effects of the oral medications. Women should discuss the pros and cons of all the available treatments with their doctors before making a decision, as new studies may reveal new options and new concerns. For some women, a non-medical option, such as a dab of K-Y Jelly or other lubricant, helps to get the natural juices flowing, as does regular sexual stimulation.

Men, Aging, and Sexuality

Men appear to be the more delicate sex in some ways. Unlike women, who experience little sexual impairment with age, a majority of men suffer prostate enlargement, a nuisance that may cause slow, frequent, and sometimes painful urination. The prostate is a small gland that encircles part of the urethra, and it is the urethra through which both the urine and semen pass. The risk of prostate cancer becomes greater with age, although this cancer is often very slow growing and causes no obvious problems. Removal of the prostate gland and reduction of its enlargement are both fairly common procedures, but they often leave patients fearing that their sexual activity has ended. In reality, while prostate surgery has risks, many men continue to enjoy vigorous sexual activity post-operatively.

Many high blood pressure medications, sedatives, hypnotics, and other tranquilizing drugs cause reduced libido, impotence, or erectile dysfunction. Men—and women, too—should ask their doctors about medicines without these side effects. Often, though, the cause is psychological rather than physical. Most specialists believe that the fear of impotence is self-fulfilling, and that the effect of the mind on the body is of great importance. Whether the problem is psychological or physical, a number of medical techniques are available to help, including penile injections, implants, pumps, and most especially, the drugs Viagra, Levitra, and Cialis.

Since Viagra's introduction to the American public in 1998, millions of prescriptions have been sold, and other drugs of its kind are now also available. Unfortunately, these drugs do not work for everyone. Men using nitrate drugs to control angina are strongly discouraged from using them. For millions of men, though—including some who have had radical prostate surgery and those taking antidepressants such as Prozac—these drugs have been successful in restoring sexual potency.

Viagra, Levitra, and Cialis work by restoring blood flow to the penis. They are not aphrodisiacs and will not create desire where none exists. Viagra's effects last for about four hours, while the effects of the other drugs can last for up to thirty-six hours, giving couples a wider window of opportunity and allowing them to be more spontaneous in their lovemaking. Like all powerful prescription drugs, these medications have side effects. Before using them, discuss their potential side effects with a physician.

SMART SEX

Along with restored sexual potency, medical authorities say that Viagra, Levitra, and Cialis have also brought with them a rise in the cases of sexually transmitted diseases, usually referred to as STDs, among people fifty and above. The drugs themselves are not the problem, of course. Rather, newly divorced or widowed men and women reentering the dating scene after many years of monogamy are finding themselves falling victim to a range of STDs that were, in former times, either unknown or more common among younger people. It is not that these people are behaving foolishly. Rather, after years of an exclusive relationship, they are simply not thinking about the risks associated with the behavior the medications allow them to enjoy.

STDs are infections that are transmitted from one person to another through sexual contact. Some of these diseases are incurable, although rarely are they deadly. Genital herpes is one such condition, and you'll sometimes, but not always, see this condition divulged in personal advertisements and profiles, so that only similarly affected people will respond.

AIDS (as well as HIV, the virus responsible for AIDS) is still incurable, although somewhat manageable, in most cases, with costly medicines. It has proven to be deadly, and it continues to spread throughout the community.

You can never assume that a person is uninfected, and if you engage in sexual intercourse, you will be safer—but not absolutely *safe*—using a latex condom. A condom can break, in which case diseases such as HIV, gonorrhea, and syphilis can be transmitted. Present knowledge is that AIDS is transmitted only when certain bodily fluids—semen or blood, for example—are exchanged. AIDS is not transmitted by casual kissing, or even by deep kissing. However, oral sex remains risky, and some STDs can be transmitted this way.

But what is a woman to do if the man can't sustain the necessary erection to use a condom? Insist that he have an HIV test! Be warned that the test is actually for the antibodies to the virus, and antibodies do not develop until six to twelve weeks after infection. This means that a person can test negative, yet can infect a sexual partner. The only way to be sure that a negative result is correct is to be celibate during the twelve-week "window period" before taking the test.

A man has the right to insist that a woman take an HIV test, too. Only you know what you have been up to sexually, and given these dangerous times, such a request is smart, not unreasonable. And it does not cast aspersions on your character. The likelihood that a woman will transmit the disease to a man is much less than the reverse, but it is still a possibility.

According to a report in the *AARP Bulletin*, Americans over fifty should pay more attention to the AIDS epidemic, as more than 10 percent of infected Americans are in that age group. At highest risk are persons who use intravenous drugs, have multiple sex partners, or have a partner who practices unsafe sex or uses drugs. But according to the article, "Other Americans over fifty are potentially at risk, sometimes without realizing it, when they begin dating following a divorce or the death of a spouse."

A survey by epidemiologist Ron Stall of the University of California at San Francisco and his colleague Joe Catania found that older Americans are one-sixth as likely as younger people to use condoms and one-fifth as likely to be tested for HIV, as they perceive themselves as not being at risk. This misconception can have serious consequences.

According to an article in *PhillyBurbs.com*, the Pennsylvania State Health Department reports that in 2002, in one county alone, 110 men and 160 women aged sixty-five and older were diagnosed with chlamydia, forty-four men and thirty-two women were diagnosed with gonorrhea, and forty-six men and women combined were diagnosed with syphilis. Between 1980 and 2004, in Bucks and Montgomery counties, 112 people aged fifty and older in each county were diagnosed with AIDS. Florida, with a retired population even greater than that of Pennsylvania, is experiencing similar numbers.

Jean's Story

Among some people, AIDS awareness is high, as is shown by "Jean's" story.

"I was seeing this nice man. We'd been out several times, and I invited him to my house for a home-cooked meal. I also invited "Peggy," my twenty-eight-year-old, unmarried daughter who lives nearby, to join us.

"My daughter saw the man reaching across the table to squeeze my hand—his way of complimenting the chef, I suppose—and, jumping to entirely the wrong conclusion, she blurted out, 'I hope you guys are using condoms. These days, you can't be too careful.' The man was absolutely mortified. He turned beet red and muttered, 'Oh, Jeez!'

"I could hardly contain myself, and as soon as he'd left the house, I burst out laughing, thinking about the poor guy's discomfort and the whole role-reversal thing—having my daughter talk to us like a parent—not that my mother or father would have *dreamed* of talking to me and a boyfriend like that! It also made me realize that younger single people take sex for granted in a way I never did—or could!"

You should never take casual sex "for granted," but if you are contemplating a new sexual relationship, you really *can't* be too careful. While AIDS can be deadly, other sexually transmitted diseases, such as herpes, gonorrhea, and chlamydia, can be devastating. Have regular medical checkups and frank discussions with your gynecologist about your sexual activity and ways to stay healthy. You can also find a wealth of information about the signs and symptoms of sexually transmitted diseases and ways of protecting yourself in the books recommended in "Useful Resources" on page 178.

"It's all very well," I can hear you say, "insisting that a man use a condom or be tested for HIV, but how am I to do that?"

Perhaps you would rather be "spontaneous," letting a kiss lead to a caress, then to another caress, and finally to bed. But this is not the time to leave things to chance or to be coy, no matter how shy or embarrassed you feel about raising the issue of protection. Young people have some bold slogans. "No glove, no love!" is one of them. You don't have to be quite as forthright, but it is perfectly acceptable to mention the dangers and to suggest that both of you need to be protected.

BEING—AND HAVING—AN UNDERSTANDING AND SENSITIVE SEX PARTNER

The long-married widow or divorcée may feel particularly vulnerable to what she sees as "predatory" males—wolves who take advantage of women—when she begins dating for the first time since her teens or twenties. She may worry that her body is unattractive and unsexy, and that she will somehow be humiliated if she opens herself to a sexual encounter. She may not understand that older men are just as vulnerable and may be equally afraid of sexual failure and rejection.

Despite their dash and bravado—after all, men are supposed to do the wooing and pursuing—older men may need a lot of verbal and physical encouragement if they are to be sexually satisfied and satisfy their partners. Concerned as they are with getting and maintaining an erection, some men may not understand the delicacy needed in approaching a new love partner. Concerns about erectile dysfunction haunt all men, almost all of whom have experienced some inability to perform sexually at some point in their lives.

In the delightful film *The Cemetery Club*, Sam Katz, a widower played by Danny Aiello, after ardently courting a widow, Esther, for several weeks, asks her if she would like him to stay the night. The push of uncertainty and embarrassment and the pull of desire that Esther feels are real and endearing, familiar to any woman who has been in her situation. The two climb the stairs to the bedroom, but then just stare at the bed in which Esther slept with her beloved husband for forty years.

Sam quickly closes the door—and drives Esther away to a hotel. Sam's understanding and gentle lovemaking indicate a delicate sensitivity to the situation that one hopes all lovers might display.

Ideally, lovers of any age try to accommodate the sexual needs and preferences of their partners, but good loving takes time, as several of my male interviewees told me. Long-married couples sometimes forget how long it was before they achieved mutual satisfaction. One woman confessed that it wasn't until two years after her wedding that she experienced her first orgasm. Another woman told me how she had resisted oral sex for more than ten years, "even though my husband longed to kiss me all over and said I was beautiful 'down there.' I thought that sex organs were ugly and dirty, and that there was something wrong with him for wanting that." Other women long to be made love to in that intimate way. "I'd read about it in stories, of course," one widow said, "and wished I could have that experience, but Frank would *never* do that. He didn't think decent women would want that, or that they would do it to their husbands. He thought only prostitutes and 'loose' women would even *know* about such things."

Alan and Liza's Story

When "Alan" and "Liza" met, they were immediately attracted to each other due to their shared interests in science and politics. Alan, divorced for several years, appeared to be emotionally well balanced, and Liza, a widow, had no doubt their lives together would be interesting and exciting. During their courtship, Liza found Alan's old-world respect charming. She expected him to kiss her at the end of their first date, as was usual with most of the men she met, but instead, he politely shook her hand. After their third meeting, she leaned forward and kissed *him*, which he seemed to appreciate. The next time, he made the first move. He was a gentle, sweet lover, kissing her and stroking her body, but he made no move to consummate their relationship sexually. As time passed, Alan found the courage to confess that since his bitter divorce, he could rarely attain or maintain an erection. He had been so hurt by his ex-wife's betrayal that he had not dated in the several years prior to meeting Liza. He feared that his ability to satisfy a woman was gone.

Liza—whose long, happy marriage to a lusty, down-to-earth fellow had in no way prepared her for this particular problem—tried not to show her dismay. "I'm sure it's like getting back on a horse when you've been thrown," she assured him. They both laughed at her unwittingly inelegant comparison. Liza whinnied to keep the mood light, but Alan doubted the solution was easy—and it wasn't.

Liza worked—and it *was* work—with Alan for almost a year to help build his trust, defuse his unresolved anger about his divorce, and release him from his fear of rejection. In cases such as Alan's, therapy is usually advised, but his antipathy to therapists, based on past experience, ruled out that option.

Liza soldiered on, listening carefully to Alan's hints, gradually discovering the kinds of touches that encouraged an erection and learning ways to reassure him of her love when the erection disappeared. She had not known that some men's nipples are as sensitive to stimulation as women's, and that the kind of kissing and suckling she enjoyed herself produced good results in Alan. She also learned that direct stimulation of his penis helped his condition. After an hour or two of this one-sided exercise, they were often both exhausted. Alan would declare that he was neglecting Liza's needs, and that he would never again be the man he once had been. "Don't worry!" she would say to ease the tension. "My turn will come!"

Her nurturing eventually produced the desired results, and it was time for her to enjoy the fruits of her labors. Alan, however, constantly analyzed his feelings and fears before, during, and after every lovemaking session, unable to let go of his residual concerns.

"This is supposed to be *fun!*" Liza would complain. "Lighten up! Be happy!" Many more months passed before Alan was completely free of his anguish and the couple finally achieved a mutually satisfying sexual relationship.

Ruth and Max's Story

"Ruth" and "Max's" problem was quite different. Max's sexual appetite needed no stimulation at all. A widower for two years, he had longed to find a permanent relationship and have the loving intimacy and kind of energetic sex life he had known with his wife of over thirty years. Ruth, widowed for several years, had not particularly missed the sexual side of marriage after her husband had died. She and her late husband had enjoyed what she considered a "normal" amount of sex that had, over time, diminished from once or twice a week to once or twice a month.

Max insisted on intercourse every night he was with Ruth, and although she protested, she gave in to his demands. She did not find the sex especially satisfying, but she was in love with Max and wanted to make him happy. The matter came to a head when they went on a European vacation together. The flight from Seattle had been draining, and Ruth collapsed into bed as soon as they checked into their Paris hotel. In no time at all, Max shook her awake, determined to "make love."

Tired and dazed from the journey and lacking sleep, Ruth's repressed anger boiled over. She leaped out of bed and shouted, "How can you be so selfish? This is *my* body, and I won't let you use it whenever you feel like it. This is *my* body!" she repeated, and burst into tears.

"I know it's your body, Ruthie," he answered quietly, "yours to do with whatever you like. But I need release. I need it every night. And if you won't give it to me, our relationship is off."

Ruth could hardly believe what she had heard. "That's emotional blackmail," she gasped, when she had recovered her breath. "If this is really the way you think of me, I don't want anything more to do with you. I'd be out of my mind to continue with you."

She crawled back into bed and, bone-weary, soon fell into a fitful sleep. Here they were on vacation in Paris, one of the most romantic cities in the world, and they were barely speaking to each other. Common sense—and true affection for each other—came to their rescue. Max, now totally deprived of sex, realized that his demands had been unreasonable, and that although Ruth had catered to him, he had not been mindful of her needs. They began talking again, and touching, and working on a plan. Sex was to be something other than merely "release"—a term Ruth found offensive—for Max, and nightly intercourse was no longer to be taken for granted.

Sex three times a week was a bit less than Max liked and a bit more than Ruth wanted, but they both knew they must compromise if they were to stay together. Max became determined to make lovemaking so enjoyable for Ruth that she might sometimes add a fourth—or even a fifth—night to their agreement!

SEXUAL INTERCOURSE VERSUS LOVEMAKING

Given the varied backgrounds, life histories, and expectations of couples coming together in their later years, it isn't surprising that they so often misunderstand and misread each other. Men and women of all ages often don't understand each other's needs and tend to see sexual activity from different perspectives.

Many men think sexual intercourse is all that sexual activity is about. Some women are not as interested in sexual intercourse as they are in being touched and stroked and caressed, and in being told that they are precious, important, and loved. These women are not "frigid" and they do enjoy making love, which they may see as separate from "sex." It is important that their partners understand this.

Both sexes say that they do things to their lovers that they would like done to themselves, but that these broad hints are not always acted upon. "I wish he would kiss my entire *back*—from the top of my spine all the way down to my toes," said one woman I interviewed. "I shower him with little kisses. I do that to him, and he loves it! But he seems to think that lapping at my clitoris is going to bring me to all kinds of ecstasy. He heads down there before I'm even warmed up. It just makes me sore after a time, especially direct, hard tonguing at the head instead of gentle licking at the sides. And when I ask him to stop, he gets upset and feels rejected and says I make him feel inadequate because he can't satisfy me."

Such a lack of understanding can be frustrating and demonstrates the need to talk about what pleases and what doesn't. Few people, however, are comfortable making specific requests. Expressing, or even thinking, negative thoughts such as, "You're in your sixties—how can you have learned so little in all those years?" is likely to bring forth that standard male response, "I've never had any complaints before!" The frustrated woman is left feeling guilty for not having orgasm after wild orgasm—the only way, it sometimes seems, for a woman to make a man feel good about his sexual prowess.

A seventy-year-old widow told me that the man with whom she is very much in love is unable, because of radical prostate cancer surgery, to have sexual intercourse, but that this in no way diminishes his ability to satisfy her completely. "When we are together, he's making love to me all day," she says. "He kisses my hands, he puts an arm around me, he touches my face in a most intimate way. He strokes my hair. By the time we go to bed, I'm already warmed up, all the juices flowing! He soon learned how to use his hands and his mouth to bring me to orgasm, and this gives him as much pleasure as it gives me."

POSITION'S THE THING

"Being potent" for a man is generally understood to include having an erection, intercourse, orgasm, and ejaculation, in that order. Yet, men tell me they can be greatly satisfied even when one or two of these elements is missing or the elements occur in a different order. For instance, older men are much slower in attaining an erection than younger men. This disadvantage, however, is offset by their ability to hold an erection longer once it is achieved. In some cases, although they "feel" an erection in their brains, the erection isn't evident where it counts! An understanding and patient partner can help a man to "grow," and that may not happen until actual intercourse. This can be a tricky problem, especially at the beginning of a sexual relationship, when neither partner knows what to expect. The man is aware of what he is feeling or not feeling, knows his history, worries about poor performance and rejection, and so guarantees failure. The woman lies there feeling unattractive and totally lacking in sex appeal.

Can a couple have sexual intercourse if the man does not have an erection or is only slightly erect? In many cases, the answer is yes, but face-to-face positions may not work as well for these men as entry from the rear.

I can hear women all over the country making sounds of dismay, and even horror, at this prospect! "This is what animals do!" is a common response when "rear entry," or "doggy position," is mentioned. Some women think it means anal intercourse, which it certainly does not. Sex expert Alex Comfort, author of *The Joy of Sex*, has long recommended rear entry, especially for post-menopausal women whose vaginas have begun to atrophy and for overweight or slightly disabled people, among others. While rear entry is not one of the more common positions for sexual intercourse—some estimates are that around 16 percent of couples use it—it can be gentle on a woman, once the technique is understood, and entry can be made with very little erection or no erection at all. According to Comfort, it can cure partial impotence or nervousness on the man's part by restoring morale. *Before* the position is understood, however, it may cause embarrassment, as well as pain in the back for the woman, who may also find her face buried uncomfortably in the mattress or the pillow!

Entry can be made either with the man kneeling behind the woman or with both partners lying on their sides, the man curled around his lover's back (the "lazy position"). Couples can experiment until they find what is best for them. Once inside the vagina, a penis can grow quite large and firm, and the man can proceed at his own pace to orgasm, with or without ejaculation. A man's ejaculate is much sparser in the later years and his orgasm is sometimes "dry," especially if he indulges in lovemaking frequently.

Rear entry does allow a man to manually stimulate the woman, but whether or not the woman achieves orgasm in that position, she will enjoy the lovemaking and will enjoy her lover's pleasure. One woman confided that after intercourse, during which her lover, in his seventies, had a "sensational" orgasm, she experienced a prolonged "sweetness" all over her lower body. "It was a kind of *bliss*, a heavenly, floating sensation, and it lasted for hours, for as long as he remained inside me, which was most of the night. It was far better than orgasm, which is over in seconds, yet it was a kind of orgasm. Gentle and diffused. It was wonderful!"

I learned from several other women that they aren't as desperate to achieve orgasm as their men seem to think they should be. They don't deny that orgasms are important—they can be a wonderful release—but they know it just may take time for their lovers to understand their bodies. Once a man brings a woman to orgasm, it becomes ever easier for him to repeat the performance. In the meantime, women tell me, they are often able to produce their own orgasms, either manually or using a vibrator. What a lover can give them besides an orgasm—or instead of it—is intimacy, closeness, warmth, tenderness, and a sense of security.

No sensible person would suggest limiting the positions used for intercourse to rear entry. Use any position that is comfortable and pleasurable. Lying face to face, with either partner on top, or curling around each other, side by side, tummy to tummy, can be delightful and can greatly enhance feelings of caring and intimacy.

One fact of life, it seems, is that what works like a charm one time may not work at all the next time. One interviewee reported, "That evening, she was absolutely carried away by the greatest passion you can imagine as I gently stroked her breasts. The next time, I couldn't arouse her at all that way. Or *any* way I tried. Women!"

Lovemaking is an ever-changing experience, a continuing experiment. Trying different kinds of touches—feather-light touches, tiny pinches and nibbles, a leisurely head-to-toe massage with baby oil—keeps the excitement alive and new. This works for long-time partners as well as for new lovers. Take a bubble bath together. Make love by candlelight. Snuggle down on cushions in front of a log fire.

Try anything and everything to see what works best. If your imaginations run dry, you might pick up some ideas from erotic videotapes or DVDs made especially for the over-forty set. While it might seem a little embarrassing or even intimidating to buy an erotic video, calling an 800 number or going to a website can certainly make such a purchase less stressful. See Useful Resources on page 177 for some recommendations for obtaining these videos.

If you are fortunate enough to live in a warm climate, why not enjoy a hot tub together under the stars? Above all, *talk* to your partner about what pleases you and what doesn't. Be willing to try new experiences, but know that you don't have to do anything you don't want to do. And be kind. Giving is also receiving.

Part of the joy of talking with women and men in their fifties through their nineties is the realization that sexual pleasure is a gift for life. Human beings are both sensual and sexual creatures whose lives are enhanced and enriched by demonstrations of caring, touching, and holding, and whose libidos need not disappear with age.

Only a few of the men with whom I spoke used chemical enhancements, such as Viagra, although some expressed curiosity about them and felt they might try one at some later date. Most of them were philosophical about the gradual lessening of their libidos as they moved into their late fifties or sixties. They, and the women in their lives, seemed to accept that at this time of their lives, unlike in their more sexually driven days, they had the time to take their lovemaking slowly and could prolong their delight in each other in ways not previously possible.

8

Reality Check

*T*hroughout this book, I have been urging you to be realistic. We all have our dreams and our fantasies, but if we cling to unreasonable expectations, we are bound for disappointment. My hope is that you will find the self-confidence you need to face the new world of dating, that you will experiment with some of the suggestions I've given you, and that you will begin to meet compatible people whose company you enjoy.

At this point, you may be starting to consider other questions. For example, are you being realistic in your search for a mate? Is time "running out" for you? Is living together a bad idea?

ABOUT LOVE AT FIRST SIGHT

Attraction to another person is exciting. It gets the juices flowing. However, it may have little to do with love. Sexual compatibility can be a wonderful comfort, a reminder and an enrichment of your identity as a woman, but it isn't love. You may think yourself "in love," but you know that love that lasts is based on much more than physical attraction and sexual satisfaction.

This in no way denies that what we used to call "an affair" can be delightful and fulfilling for some people. In her book *The Late Show*, Helen Gurley Brown urges older women to remain sexually active even if it means having sex with some other woman's "mildly unhappy" husband! Sex is separate from love, she writes, and sex with a man, even if you aren't aflame with desire, keeps you "womanly." When Brown was asked how she would feel if she discovered *her* husband was serving another woman in this way, she answered that she would kill him!

One of the risks of having an affair, even if your partner is not married to someone else, is that you may find yourself fantasizing that it is "true love." If both partners are realistic, they can enjoy themselves for as long as the affair lasts and not suffer too much emotional damage when it comes to an end. They might even remain friends. All too often, one partner becomes more emotionally involved than the other. That partner constantly waits for declarations of commitment, which never come, and finally becomes badly hurt. If the man *is* married, you have another set of problems.

"Look," I can hear you protest, "I don't want to have an affair, or a succession of affairs, even if I know that's what they are and can keep cool about them. I'm looking for a partnership that will last."

First, then, forget the idea that you will know at first glance that you have met your mate! Not long ago, I was given the pleasant task of writing staff "profiles" for a company's in-house newsletter. In large, bureaucratic organizations, staff members often have no idea what roles their co-workers play in the company, and they certainly don't know much about their personal lives, hobbies, or interests. In my interviews, I learned each person's marital status, and I asked the married people for brief histories of their courtships. Whirlwind, swept-off-your-feet romances? There were none!

One woman who had only recently married had known her husband for twenty-two years! They had been college sweethearts for four years and then went their separate ways for twelve years before meeting up again. It was another five years before they realized they were "meant for each other."

Another woman, whose passion was dancing, first met her fiancé in a dance class, then later at a dance club. However, it was several years before they found they made beautiful music together.

Yet another staff person, planning to marry "before too long," had known his fiancée for four years before deciding she was "the one." Instant love is a bit like "overnight stardom" in show business.

These people all knew that it takes time—although not necessarily several years—for two people to understand each other well enough to make their way together through the thick and thin of everyday life.

BE REALISTIC IN YOUR SEARCH

Being realistic about a potential partner means using the wisdom you have gained over the years to resist setting impossible standards. Certainly, you may have a "wish list," but you are mature enough to know that no one person can be expected to meet all your needs. You know that you are not perfect either and will not live up to another person's every expectation.

Allow yourself and others to be human. This does not mean accepting someone as a partner if he does not enrich and enhance your life in important ways. It does mean getting rid of the romantic fantasies that no one can fulfill, to prevent yourself from being disappointed.

REEVALUATE YOUR NEEDS

Searching for someone new after years of happiness—or unhappiness—with a former husband or lover may mean taking a long, clear look at your present circumstances and, perhaps, broadening the range of men you consider acceptable. Don't deny yourself opportunities to meet fine men from walks of life other than your own. Although your first husband might have been a lawyer, your next husband could be a chef or a carpenter.

If you thought you were attracted only to men who work with their hands, you might be surprised to find yourself falling for a journalist or a teacher. If the most important item on your wish list is "academic background and the ability to discuss the philosophies of Hegel and Wittgenstein," clearly you are substantially limiting your options. Perhaps you need to rethink the likelihood of meeting such a person in your age range who is also single, who can dance a fancy fandango (another item on your wish list), and who will be bowled over by what you have to offer.

Ask yourself if it's more important to retain or regain the "status" you enjoyed with your former husband or lover than make a good life with a man who earns, or earned, his living in a more humble job or trade. Only you can decide how important this is to you. Chances are that if you really want to find a new partner, you will need to feed your intellectual appetite through a university course or your ballroom desires through a dance class, and modify your expectations.

A *Los Angeles Times* article written by Janet Kinosian examines successful couples whose tastes in leisure activities ran so counter to each other's that a computer matchmaking program would have "spit the two in opposite directions." In one case, the husband loved opera and studied foreign languages, while the wife adored watching television soaps and reading "bodice rippers." Other couples differed even more in their ideas of how to spend their spare time and in the kinds of vacations they enjoyed.

All these happily married couples had adjusted their expectations of each other, often taking separate vacations and allowing each other plenty of "personal space." They realized that it was far better for a husband to trek through the wilderness with only the knapsack on his back—if that's what refreshed him and gave him the energy to go back to his twelve-hour work days—than to expect him to accompany his wife to Las Vegas and spend long days and nights at the gaming tables—if that's what pleased *her*. They learned that neither partner should sacrifice his or her own enjoyment for the other's, and that it is not necessary for couples to march in lockstep through every activity in order to be happy together. Each can agree to be different without loving the other less.

Good, kind, generous, loving, faithful, understanding men can be found in all occupations. Their interests and hobbies outside their work run the gamut, from baseball to Bach. Being realistic does not mean "lowering your standards." At the same time, women who were married to working men need not feel that business and professional men are "above them."

Women who restrict themselves to a narrow segment of the population may be making a real mistake. "Jim," one of the most interesting men I know, has been an electrician for much of his working life, was a union organizer in his youth, worked for civil rights in the sixties, loves classical music and jazz, and teaches tai chi in his spare time! Regardless of her background, a woman would not be lowering her standards in any way by becoming Jim's partner.

MOVE AT YOUR OWN PACE

Let us pretend that you know Jim. You met him on a hike, or through a personal advertisement, or at a meeting of your local political club. He's a nice man whose heart is in the right place, no question about it. He is concerned about the state of the world, follows political events, and plays an active part in registering voters. You like him and admire him. And yet . . .

What do you do if a really fine man like Jim is clearly interested in you and soon begins talking about a possible future together? While his attention warms and comforts you, you don't feel the kind of affection he feels for you.

An old song goes, "A good man nowadays is hard to find," and those words are just as true now as when they were written. You don't want to lose a good man, yet you are not ready—and may never be ready—to be more than friends with him.

Give yourself—and him—a chance! Let him know that you care about him, and that you appreciate his feelings for you, but that you are not ready to take the serious step of agreeing to share your life with him. Don't allow yourself to be rushed or pushed into any commitment you may regret.

Jim may not want to wait. His affection for you may cool, and your decision will be made for you. You'll both move on. On the other hand, he may feel so strongly about you that he is willing to take the chance that, sooner or later, you will begin to care for him the same way he cares for you.

Months later, Jim's courtship of you bears fruit. You realize that he has become central to your life, and that most of the plans you make and almost every outing you consider includes him and would be empty without him. You are becoming a couple.

The other possibility is that you will grow apart. Even though you may still think of Jim as a good person, you may begin to find that you are relieved when he leaves your house and you can relax with a good book or attend a play by yourself. You may want to plan a trip without him because you think two weeks of close proximity would be overpowering. Time may have done its work.

Still, be sure it is really over before you release Jim to some other woman who might appreciate him more than you do. Even the most solid partnerships have emotional ebbs and flows. If pressed, most happily married people will admit to times when they would like to be alone, when the strain of domestic life becomes overwhelming and they envy their single friends. Perhaps this restlessness you feel is just part of a normal emotional cycle and will pass.

Remember that adapting to life with another person is easier when you are young and just starting out together. Your tastes and attitudes develop as you spend days and years in each other's company, and you get to know each other's funny little ways over time. In a good marriage of many years or decades, you agree to disagree. You learn flexibility. You learn to overlook the other's funny little quirks and perhaps even begin to hardly notice them any longer.

At age sixty or more, you each have had a lifetime of separate experiences. You have become the person you are without any input from the person you are considering as a partner for the remainder of your life. You may find some of each other's habits irritating, and you may worry that they will become unbearable.

Still, don't give up too quickly. Take a little break and go by yourself on that trip for a couple of weeks. If you soon yearn to see him, you may be more ready to make a commitment than you thought. If the time you spend on your own brings nothing but relief, make your farewells and start keeping an eye open for someone more compatible.

YOU DO HAVE ENOUGH TIME

Finding the right partner, like many important things in life, can take time, perhaps a long time. "But I'm sixty-two now," I can hear you say. "Next year, I'll be sixty-three. Time is not on my side."

Men and women in their thirties and forties often have the same lament. People of all ages meet and fall in love, and while "time is of the essence" for women nearing the end of their childbearing years, it is not a problem for the over-fifty crowd.

Jerry's Story

My good friend "Jerry" had been actively searching for the right woman for about four years, since about a year after his wife died. Retired, he had plenty of time to explore a number of avenues. His personal advertisement appeared week after week, month after month, in the local newspaper. He advertised in magazines with editorial views in tune with his own. He went to discussion groups, and he organized his own salons. He took courses, met and dated dozens of women, and generally enjoyed himself.

At times, though, he confided that he was getting really weary of the dating game. The more ladies he dated, the more difficult it became for him to make a decision. Many of the women he met were delightful. "I like this one's sense of humor, that one's beautiful smile, that one's lovely voice, this one's intelligence . . ." he would say. But he couldn't seem to find everything he wanted in just one of them.

Then six months ago, "Joyce" responded to his newspaper advertisement, and Jerry is now on Cloud Nine! He says he feels about this elegant and gracious lady as he has never felt about anyone before. He has met enough women by this time to know that some qualities are more important to him than others. Luckily for him, Joyce cares for him as much as he cares for her. Jerry is seventy-eight years old. I have never heard him refer to his age as any kind of handicap to finding a suitable partner.

While on jury duty not long ago, I made friends with a fellow juror, a middle-aged woman with teenage children who had recently remarried after many years as a divorcée. She told me with a smile on her face that her mother, who is in her early seventies, was *also* newly married, to a man several years younger than herself, her first husband having died three years earlier.

Gillian's Story

"Gillian," one of my oldest friends (I've known her some thirty years), had a close liaison with "Bob" for over fifteen years. They had met soon after her second divorce, and although she cared for Bob, with her past bad experience with marriage she was not eager to marry him or even to live with him. They kept separate homes in the same town, but spent all their leisure time together, including taking numerous long trips abroad.

Recently, Gillian met "Philip"—at a party she attended with Bob— and the two found they had a lot to talk about together. At the moment, Gillian is dating both Bob and Philip, and both men are fully aware of the situation. Bob, seeing the way Philip is pursuing Gillian, is pressing hard for marriage. Philip is attentive and generous, and is also pressing for marriage. Gillian is having a wonderful time being courted by two highly eligible men. Is she young and glamorous? She is in her mid-sixties and is nice looking, but she is not particularly a beauty.

YOU WILL HAVE DRY SPELLS

Be prepared, too, for dry spells—perhaps lasting several months—when you meet no eligible men at all. If you are involved in activities for the pleasure they give you rather than only as opportunities for finding a partner, you will enjoy yourself anyway and will come away enriched. Part of this enrichment may result from finding people with interests similar to yours and, in the process, making new friends. I have added several wonderful women to my circle of friends, meeting them at conversation groups and singles events that I was researching as possible resources for people looking for partners.

LIVING TOGETHER: GOOD IDEA OR BAD?

Your feelings about the morality of living with a member of the opposite sex without the benefit of marriage are for you to sort through. As far as society is concerned, the arrangement is now commonplace, with most of the debate over the issue centering on what to call the "roommate." "Significant other?" "Posslque (Person of the Opposite Sex Sharing Living Quarters)?" "Lover?" Playwright Rochelle Newman uses the term "spousal equivalent" and jokes that living together is the Nutrasweet version of marriage. "He has all the great taste of a husband, but only half the commitment." Young people often live together for a year or two before marriage, although contrary to belief, research indicates that couples living together beforehand have slightly higher rates of divorce than couples who did not live together before marriage.

One internationally known matchmaker strongly advises against living together if you really want marriage. Of course, there is often a solid reason *not* to marry—perhaps one of the parties will lose a pension or some other form of income. Otherwise, she asks, why would your partner marry you if he essentially has you as a wife without the commitment involved in declaring your association formally and legally?

More importantly, why settle for living together if what you really want is marriage, since living together does not particularly prepare you for or lead you to marriage? Do you really want to give up your own home and your chance of meeting a serious marriage partner just on the hope that the relationship will be permanent? Perhaps it will last as long as you do, but if it fails, you may lose a great deal emotionally and, perhaps, financially as well.

According to Linda Stern, writing in *Modern Maturity*, "what's mine isn't necessarily yours" when it comes to couples who live together. She cites Mark and Alice as a couple with unequal incomes. Mark was well-to-do and retired, while Alice was still working and earning a modest salary. Their relationship fell apart because Mark expected Alice to cater to his expensive tastes on her limited budget. Financial planners urge couples to avoid such unhappy endings by discussing financial arrangements before they move in together. Unmarried couples are also encouraged to keep their finances separate.

Further, in the event that your live-in partner dies before you, will you be homeless if the house was his and has been willed to his heirs? It is wise for you to seek legal advice before setting up home with anyone, but *especially* before moving in with someone to whom you are not married.

MARRIAGE WITHOUT LOVE

In our society, we believe so firmly in the notion of romantic love that we forget, if we ever knew, that marriages at one time were—and still are, in some cultures—arranged for practical reasons rather than for passion. These transactions, based on family connections, financial interests, and sometimes simple convenience, appear to have been no less successful than matches based on romantic attraction. In time, the people involved often came to care deeply for one another, even though they were not expected to be "in love" when they said their marriage vows. This is shown beautifully in *Fiddler on the Roof*, when Tevye begins to think about his relationship with his wife, Golda. Their lovely duet begins when Tevye asks his wife if she loves him. She looks at him as though he's crazy and proceeds to list everything she has done for him over the years, including cooking for him, cleaning for him, and bearing his children. He continues to ask her if she loves him, and finally, although Golda never actually says those words, Tevye concludes that she really does.

Approximately 50 percent of marriages today end in divorce, even though they were likely entered into with great love and high expectations. Perhaps some thought should be given to marriage founded on practical considerations.

Before you shake your head right off your shoulders, consider the people for whom a sensibly realistic union might work, even if you have never thought of such a marriage for yourself.

Grace and Gregory's Story

"Grace" owns the house in which she and her first husband reared their children. When her husband died five years ago, their insurance paid off the mortgage. However, the household expenses were still a struggle for her to meet on her pension, and she found the property difficult to maintain by herself. Her husband used to look after the garden and the cars, while she did the housework and the interior decorating. After his death, she sometimes felt overwhelmed by the responsibility of caring for everything. She occasionally used a handyman and a gardener, but she worried about the costs of these services.

Grace had considered selling the house and renting a small apartment, or moving to a less expensive, more manageable house, but both these options depressed her. She had lived in her house for thirty years and was comfortable there, knew and liked her neighbors, and did not want to face what she saw as a horrible upheaval of her life.

"Gregory," retired on a small company pension and social security payments, was divorced nearly twenty years ago. He had entered into several "relationships" after the divorce, but none had satisfied him for long. He did not particularly enjoy life on his own, although he had become quite good at cooking, shopping, and cleaning. He lived in a small apartment and worried as the rent increased steadily over the years while his income shrank.

Gregory had not been "seeing" anyone for several years when he met Grace. They were both lonely. Grace felt she was fading away, missing her life companion and her two grown children, both of whom lived and worked on the other side of the country. She volunteered some time to a local organization working with handicapped children, and it was through this agency that she met Gregory, who was also trying to expand his horizons.

They liked each other, but they did not fall crazily in love. They got along well and could be open with each other about their likes and dislikes. They both enjoyed musicals, although neither of them had much money to spare for costly theater tickets. They usually attended inexpensive events, and planned visits to local museums and galleries for days when the admission was free. They generally each paid their own way when they went to a movie or a restaurant. Grace sometimes cooked dinner for them, with Gregory bringing wine or a package of gourmet coffee for a treat.

Neither Grace nor Gregory pretended to be in love, although they soon became the best of friends and, together, eased much of each other's loneliness. They took some thrifty trips together and found they remained calm and amicable even during and after long days of driving together in a small, not particularly comfortable car. They shared motel rooms, usually with twin beds, but they did sleep in the same bed occasionally and enjoyed making love sometimes.

Grace and Gregory dated for a while, perhaps for a year or more. As each became more knowledgeable about the other's finances and living arrangements, they began having a series of "what if" discussions: "What if you sold your house and . . . ?" "What if I left my apartment and . . . ?" "What if I moved into your house and contributed my rent to our shared household . . . ?" "What if I moved in and took over the outside chores . . . ?"

After some months of debate, they decided they both required a more permanent arrangement than simply moving into the same residence and sharing expenses, although they saw that option as a sensible possibility, perhaps as a first step. Both had lived in their present homes for a long time and needed to hold on to a sense of security.

Gregory began staying over at Grace's house for long weekends and eventually for a week or two at a time. The couple was forced to work out a plan for living together. Both were private people. They each needed a place to which they could retreat for solitude. Gregory took the second bedroom as his own, using it for sleeping and as his office. Both Gregory and Grace figured they would sleep together in the master bedroom once they were married.

By the time they married, their living plan was in place. Today, they share the chores and contribute equally to the food, heating, and other household bills, reducing costs for both of them. They have more money to pay for outside services if they need them. They have companionship when they need it, privacy when they want it, and someone to "be there" if either falls sick or needs some kind of physical or emotional support. The two respect each other, like each other, care about each other, but are still not "in love."

We do not need to "fall in love" or "be in love" in order to care for someone very much and, perhaps, to eventually find that we love that other person. Love is enough of a mystery to allow for all kinds of possibilities, as those arranged marriages of the past demonstrate.

The house remains Grace's property. In her will, she has stipulated that if she dies first, Gregory may remain in the house for as long as he wishes. After he leaves or dies, her children will be able to sell the house and share the proceeds. This kind of marriage may not suit the more romantically inclined, but it is built on firm ground and is without illusions.

"What would happen," you may ask, "if either one *does* meet someone else and fall madly in love?" Grace and Gregory have talked about this possibility the same way they talk openly about any concern. They have concluded that the chances of this are slight. They are not looking outside their marriage for companionship with someone of the opposite sex. Like any couple firmly committed to each other, they have closed off that option. Each lived alone long enough to know that the comfort and security they enjoy together is precious and must not be jeopardized.

The arrangement that Grace and Gregory have designed to meet their needs is just one among many possible ways for couples to share their lives these days. As we live longer, we may become even more flexible in the living styles we consider acceptable and desirable. A soon-to-be married couple I interviewed recently plans to live much like Grace and Gregory, but the wife-to-be has clearly stipulated that the relationship will not be sexual, her husband-to-be agreeing to this restriction. To judge by their affectionate handholding, the two are dear friends. I look forward to talking to them in a year or so to see if anything has changed.

"Being realistic" doesn't mean pushing your dreams aside and settling for something you do not want. Rather, it means understanding and accepting the world as it is. "Being realistic" means keeping an open mind and taking the time to consider carefully all the possibilities that life holds for happiness.

Maturity gives us an edge. For example, we have experienced enough living to appreciate the wisdom of the following poem, *After a While* by Veronica Shoffstall, which is one of my favorites.

> After a while you learn . . .
> that love doesn't mean leaning
> and company doesn't always mean security.
>
> And you begin to learn that kisses aren't contracts
> and presents aren't promises
> and you begin to accept your defeats
> with your head up and your eyes ahead
> with the grace of a woman
> not the grief of a child.

And after a while you learn
that even sunshine burns
if you get too much
so you plant your own garden
and decorate your soul
instead of waiting for someone to bring you flowers.

And you learn
that you really can endure
that you really are strong
that you really do have worth
and you learn
and you learn
with every goodbye
you learn . . .

That's being realistic.

9

Alternatives to Marriage and "Romantic" Love

*T*he author of one how-to book on finding a husband guarantees that if you follow her advice, you will be successful within a year. Or what? You'll receive five million dollars?

You and I both know there are no guarantees in life. It is possible that you won't find your mate anytime soon. But this can happen for any number of reasons—not necessarily because, despite all efforts, the man of your dreams fails to appear. After careful consideration, for instance, you may decide that you would rather live alone. For you, the costs of permanent companionship may outweigh the rewards.

THE BENEFITS OF BEING SINGLE

Research on widowhood, published several decades ago by Helena Z. Lopata, indicated that the majority of the 254 not-remarried widows in the study, all fifty years old or older, did not wish to remarry, even when they felt that their husbands had been unusually good men. Similarly, many of the widows I interviewed were hesitant about remarriage, particularly when they had nursed a husband through a long final illness. A not unusual sentiment, perhaps a rationalization, expressed by older single women, widowed or divorced, is "I wouldn't want to end up as a nurse to a sick old man."

Such a seemingly harsh statement is often made in the abstract, when a woman isn't actually seeing someone. On the other hand, one charming widow whose husband had been confined to a wheelchair for ten years before his death, unable to walk or even stand, said, "I looked after Paul the best I could for all those years and I wouldn't hesitate to do it again for someone I love."

Although she now has an attentive lover who lives nearby, she, too, states firmly that she would not marry him, even though he proposes to her every Saturday night! Why not? Not because she fears being a caregiver to an invalid once more. Rather, she relishes the freedom from the more general domestic responsibilities that marriage would undoubtedly bring. "As things are, he takes care of his own laundry, his grocery shopping . . . and if I cook dinner, he brings wine and flowers. I like it this way. He lives close enough so I can see him whenever I want to, but I can also be independent."

Cynthia S. Smith's *Why Women Shouldn't Marry* expands on the theme of independence. The only reasons for a woman to marry are support and sperm, Smith writes. Why give up your freedom if you want or need neither? Smith's view is that women make far more sacrifices than men when they marry, and that widows, especially, should consider alternatives. "You've been through enough!" she declares.

Smith's insistence that women give more to a marriage than men, and get less in return, is supported by the classic work of sociologist Jessie Bernard. In *The Future of Marriage,* Bernard claims that every marriage consists of two marriages, his and hers, and that his is better! Married men, her studies show, live longer than unmarried men; married men are healthier than unmarried men or married women; married men express more satisfaction with their lives than do unmarried men or married women. In fact, the only group expressing more satisfaction with their lives than married men is unmarried women.

More recent studies add further support to Bernard's findings. Linda Waite, President of the Population Association of America, also finds that although the wedded state appears to be good for both sexes, women get less out of marriage than men, and that their level of sexual satisfaction does not usually rise after marriage. Married men, however, have sex twice as often as single men, and their level of satisfaction is higher than that of single men.

These general facts do not, of course, argue or suggest that marriage can never be an ideal arrangement for many women as well as for men. My own marriage, entered into when I was very young, allowed and encouraged substantial personal growth for both my husband and me. I don't think either of us could have made the progress we did without the other. We were, however, teenagers when we met. We grew up together and learned over the years to tolerate each other's funny little ways, and to ignore those behaviors that would have driven us crazy had we let them!

SUPPORT AND SPERM: DO YOU NEED THEM?

Until relatively recently, couples who fell in love expected—and were expected—to marry. Not many women earned as much as men, and few could support themselves. If women did not marry, their usual option was to remain under their parents' roof, dependent children for ever.

Falling in love, which many social scientists tell us is a social or cultural invention, provided the reason for a man and a woman to bind themselves together legally and set up a home for themselves and, before long, for their children. A woman exchanged dependency on her parents for dependency on her husband.

Although today's women still earn less than men, they need not be married to leave their parents' homes, nor do they need to depend on parental support. Further, financially independent women no longer have to stay in bad or unsatisfying marriages—which may account, at least in part, for the recent increase in late-life divorces.

Retired or working older people are even less likely than youngsters to need marriage for financial security. In fact, marriage may prove financially detrimental. In her article "Love and Money" in *Modern Maturity*, Linda Stern writes that couples who remain unmarried are spared an Internal Revenue Service "marriage penalty," which can be substantial. A widow's pension is sometimes lost if the woman remarries, as are workers' compensation benefits payable to a widow whose husband died in a work-related event. Social security benefits, too, may be reduced or lost. People considering remarriage should check carefully to determine possible losses or reductions of these kinds. Couples living together without marriage should also be sure that estate plans are clearly written to avoid possible disagreements with more traditional heirs.

True, two incomes are bigger than one, and a couple, married and both working, may be able to afford more spacious living accommodations and more material objects than a man and woman living separately. However, this fact alone may not be enough to lead a couple to marry today. And the need to have children—the only other reason besides support that Smith considers compelling enough for a woman to marry—is probably not an issue for most couples past fifty, despite the latest advances in reproductive medicine that allow women to give birth later and later in life!

Wanda Sykes, the standup comedian, voiced the same thought a little differently on the Comedy Channel's "Tongues Untied." Marriage, she says, is a business. Its product is children. If you aren't going to have children, the business goes down the tubes because there's no inventory!

THE JOYS OF INDEPENDENCE

Even some women who felt they wanted nothing more than to remarry after the death of a husband or after a divorce, find the urgency of this desire waning with time. Women may begin to appreciate the control they have over their time and money. Those who have never lived alone before are able, perhaps for the first time in their lives, to come and go as they please without telling daddy or hubby where they are going, who they are going with, and when they will be back. They can take themselves to the movies in the afternoon without having to explain their movements—without feeling guilty for being cooped up indoors when the sun is shining. They can see the movies they prefer and tune into the television programs they enjoy, rather than giving in to others' tastes and wishes. A woman may never have to watch football again unless, of course, she wants to.

Independence can be heady stuff. Assuming a woman is keeping track of income and expenditures, she may decide to buy that lovely but expensive outfit in the department store window, again without consulting her spouse, without waiting for his approval, and without his obvious disapproval when she carries her purchases home.

Seline's Story

"Seline" had been a widow for four years after a long and good marriage. She was one of those women who thought she wanted nothing other than remarriage to a man similar in temperament to her husband—if she could find him. In the past two years, she had met and dated several decent men, but none quite fit the bill. "Harry," a widower, was a decent man of similar cultural background to her own and to her late husband's. He was the first man she considered seriously as a potential mate.

For several months, Harry had been courting her patiently, ardently, caringly. He sensed her reluctance to settle down with him, even though she was, as yet, not aware of it herself. She liked his company and enjoyed his gentle sense of humor, but she found a day with him too long and a weekend *much* too long. She was relieved when he left, glad to have her house to herself again.

"I don't know what's the matter with me," she confided. "I feel so guilty. As though I'm leading him on. He's a good man; I like him very much but . . ."

Together, we probed her feelings. As Harry had to travel some distance to be with Seline, she allowed him to stay overnight at her house— not in her bed, but in the spare room. He agreed to this arrangement even though he would have preferred to sleep with her. "I don't feel ready for that, yet" she said. "It would indicate a commitment that I'm not sure I can make. And you know the way we were brought up; we don't go to bed with people we aren't really sure about."

Early in the morning after his first stopover, Harry woke her with a cup of tea, first rapping on the bedroom door to announce himself. "I know he meant well. He was trying to show me what a splendidly domestic creature he is, but I was *really* annoyed. I spent much of the day asking myself why I felt that way. After all, I often make myself an early morning cup of tea and take it back to bed with me."

She concluded that her irritation was based on being pulled out of a deep sleep—sleep that she felt she needed. She is normally an early riser, and her days are filled with strenuous activities. That morning, she happened to sleep a little longer than usual. "I know this sounds unreasonable, but how dare someone take it on himself to wake me up?"

Seline's annoyance with Harry over this small matter and other similarly trivial intrusions demonstrated that she had become used to living alone. Seline went on to say, "He picked up my crossword while I was pouring him a second cup of coffee and filled in one of the clues. It made me really angry, though I know it shouldn't have." Not only has Seline developed her own routines as a single person, but she *likes* them and resents their being ignored, even though "the poor man" can't be expected to know them unless he is told.

"It seems so unfair to expect him to fit in with *my* ways, but I like the life I've made for myself. True, I fret over the chores and all the responsibility that used to be shared, but I'm proud of the way I manage. I'm not sure I want someone telling me 'better' ways to do things."

Seline has not yet resolved the situation with Harry, but has become aware of her own uncertainty and will not rush into a marriage or other shared domestic arrangement. She is, as she says, "still evolving" as an independent human being. If Harry cares enough for her, he will continue to be patient.

Many older single men, both divorced and widowed, also prefer not to remarry, although this may not be what they say or what they want you to believe! A man who has lived on his own for ten or fifteen years—all the while declaring how much he wants to find the right woman to marry—is most unlikely to relinquish his single state.

In the early years after his wife's death or his divorce, a man may be helpless in the kitchen and hopeless with the laundry. As time passes, he learns to cook for himself—and he cooks what *he* likes the way *he* likes it! He, like his female counterpart, may find some advantages in living alone and being accountable to no one. Used to discussing a potential purchase at length with his wife—say, a new set of golf clubs or some state-of-the-art video equipment—and often being dissuaded from such an extravagance, he may now indulge himself in ways never before possible, and may not want to give up that freedom.

Many women and men, then, may conclude that living alone, while it may not be perfect and is sometimes lonely, is preferable to making the sacrifices necessary to share hearth and home with someone else.

WHAT TODAY'S WOMAN CAN TEACH US

On a recent camping trip with the Sierra Club, I met a group of women in their mid-forties to mid-fifties, whose conversation stopped me in my tracks. These women made me realize that some ways of thinking about the place of men in our lives not only may be out of date, but also may stop us from realizing our potential. Our old beliefs could be cutting us off from joys we didn't know we could experience.

Many of us grew up during a time when women who did not marry were pitied as spinsters. They were viewed, and viewed themselves, as undesirable and incomplete. A single woman was labeled an old maid as early as her late twenties. Some of us still hold this view, leading to many an interesting discussion with our daughters, who don't seem to be in any hurry to marry and give us grandchildren.

Our daughters are like those women I met climbing in the Sierras. They too came of age after the women's liberation movement of the

1970s, and have their own view of how men fit into their lives. Most young women do want children, but later on. They would like to raise these children in two-parent families.

However, the somewhat older women I met on this trip—educated women with careers—were no longer "one man away from poverty." Nor, given their age, did they need men to father their children. They enjoyed men's company, but they had learned that they don't have to live *with* them to live. It may be a lesson we can use to our advantage— a lesson that men, particularly some older men, may still have to learn.

Jeb's Story

At sixty, "Jeb" had been married for decades and had fathered three daughters, all now grown and independent. Then his wife broke it to him that she really preferred women, and that she was going off to live with one. You can imagine what this did to the poor fellow's sense of self, of masculinity, even if the marriage "hadn't been good" for some time. Jeb, a biologist, joined the Peace Corps for a couple of years to get his head straight and plan how to live the rest of his life.

When Jeb returned to the United States, he rented an apartment month to month and set three goals for himself: to find a woman to share his life; to move to a rural or semi-rural area, either in America or abroad; and to find some useful, satisfying work in his field. He gave himself eight months to accomplish all of this.

"Perhaps you should move first," I suggested, "and find a woman who is already where you think you want to live."

"Well, I've been round and round on this and I've decided to find the woman first, as there may be less selection in the place I might want to settle."

He placed a personal advertisement in his large city's newspaper: "DM. 62, well-educ, travld, fin sec, fit. ISO [in search of] romance, adventure, caring, sharing, LTR [long-term relationship]."

A few weeks after he advertised, I asked him how the search was going.

"I've given it up," he said, tersely.

"But why? What happened? How many women did you meet?"

"About a dozen. But they're all the same."

"The same? What do you mean?"

"Well, they're all intelligent, nice-looking professionals with houses and careers and . . ."

"You mean they have *lives*," I interrupted.

"Yes. And I can't believe how unadventurous they are. They have their *routines* and they expect me to just *slot into* their calendars. They aren't willing to even consider starting a new life."

"Why would they? With someone they don't even know. It takes time to make a decision like that."

"Why? It didn't take me any time. I *know* what I want."

"But you don't have anything to give up. No home, no job. Your family is scattered. You're as free as the air. These women have worked hard to establish themselves; why would they sacrifice that?"

"What sacrifice? A *house*? Things? I'm talking about building an exciting new life with someone."

Here was an educated man of pleasant enough appearance, but otherwise an unknown quantity, expecting one advertisement in the newspaper to bring him a wonderful woman. This woman would be willing to give up her hard-won security to walk into the sunset with him, hand in hand, without his making any effort to woo, to please, to win her—without taking the time to know what *she* might be seeking. He didn't understand that women today have all kinds of options, and that the men who want to be with them may, indeed, have to "slot into" their lives—if, in fact, they have a place at all.

Sandra's Story

"Sandra," one of the women in the camping group, had just sold the business she had established five years before, and knew that the gain from the sale would support her for several years. When I met her, she was weighing her choices. In her early fifties, she was fit, active, attractive, intelligent, self-sufficient, funny—and felt that she could do anything she wanted.

"The whole world is waiting for me," she said.

She might live in Tuscany for a year, study art in Paris, and purchase a round-the-world airline ticket. A man in her life? Yes, there was someone she cared for, but she had been married and divorced three times, she did not intend to have any more children, and she did not need financial support. She was free to set out on adventures she could not have considered earlier in her life.

Would her man accompany Sandra on her travels? She was not sure. She was fond of him but, "This is a most marvelous time for women in our situation," she said, almost singing the words. "We've built a circle of friends and family, and leaving them to explore some other style of life means we widen that circle still more. We add new friends, discover new ways of being. We are truly privileged."

Agreed. Still, not every woman is able or *wants* to leave her familiar life. Neither, however, need she wait for a man to come along, scoop her up, and "take her away from all this." Women are changing direction, seeking their own adventures, making decisions that may not include men at all.

FINDING A NEW MEANING IN LIFE

Finding meaning in life—a reason to start each day—is a serious pursuit for all human beings, young and old. It becomes especially important when much of what used to define us has been lost or put aside. The answer to "What do you do?" tells others who we are. It also reconfirms our own identity. Even the phrase "I'm *only* a housewife"—the slightly apologetic reply given by some people since the feminist movement encouraged women into offices and factories—reassures us that we have a "place" and a job to do.

In the later years, retirement, though it may be anticipated with pleasure, strips us of one of the more important aspects of ourselves, our status in the professional or working world. And although the housewife does not retire, she no longer has youngsters to care for. The widowed or divorced housewife cooks and cleans only for herself.

The challenge is to reinvent ourselves, to find new identities, new reasons to anticipate each day with pleasure, and new ways of loving and being loved that may, or may not, include romantic or sexual love. It may mean inventing, or becoming part of, a new "family," finding ways to be among children, or it may mean inventing a new *self*—perhaps finally *becoming* the artist or writer you've always daydreamed about, now that you are free of responsibilities for others.

Finding a New "Family"

The woman with grandchildren who live nearby is likely to have a sense of continuity with the past. She also has reason to plan ahead, and a proud and legitimate role as grandma that helps sustain her sense of self and gives her an honorable place within a family.

The current trend towards deferred parenting, especially among career-oriented couples, leaves many people without grandchildren at an age when *their* parents had grandchildren already in high school or college. My own father, for instance, was forty-four years old when his first grandson was born. Now, some men are waiting until their forties to *start* their families, and their wives are in their late thirties, even early forties, when the first child is born.

The grandparent role, then—the role most of us expected to play—may not be ours until we are quite old, if ever. And even those who *are* grandparents may live thousands of miles away from the grandchildren they seldom see.

For those who miss having children in their lives, who get dewy-eyed at the sight of a new baby, who long to hold a child or romp with children in the park or on the living room floor, the way to fill that need may be to become someone's surrogate grandparent.

Sometimes, those same children who are born late in their parents' lives, don't have any grandparents. My own research, described in my book *Last Chance Children,* has shown that such youngsters feel happier when they have older people who care about them and who "stand in" as grandparents, especially when their parents are busy professionals, as is often the case these days.

This would seem a perfect matching of needs. Look around your neighborhood. Perhaps you already know some busy parents. Talk to them, and you may find that they would love to have a nearby "grand-parent" for their children. Even if their own parents are still living, they may live far away, so your wisdom and experience may be appreciated in all kinds of ways. With luck, and after establishing mutual trust with the parents, your ready-made family will be close at hand.

Other ways of participating in the lives of children would be to give some of your time to your local kindergarten or grade school. Small children love to listen to stories and to have books read to them. And many parents, because of the demands of their jobs or careers, no longer have time for this enjoyable activity. Schools encourage—and need—the participation of people in the community as teachers' aides.

Hospitalized youngsters may need someone to sit with them and talk or gently croon, or to hold them and rock them. People who regularly help in this way tell me that the satisfaction and love they receive far outweigh the "sacrifice" of their time.

Finding Your Creative Self

Many of us who are now in our fifties and beyond grew up believing in the rightness of loving companionship. If you married and experienced the joy of partnership, of sharing life's pleasures and problems, you might now have a hard time imagining real happiness as a single individual. It's difficult to abandon the idea that you need someone else to complete you, even if your partnership was not ideal. Old habits and beliefs die hard.

Now, though, women, young and old, have given themselves "permission" to enjoy being single, to be "selfish" and to live for themselves. Alternatives to marriage or long-term relationships include the joy that comes from finding and developing your creative talents.

For most of your life, you lived through and for others. You were allowed only your spare time for your own interests—and spare time, when you are rearing a family, is a scarce commodity indeed. Now may be your time, at last, to live for yourself. And if not now, when?

Without thinking about it for too long, write down at least five answers to the following question: "If you could do anything in the world, regardless of anyone else's opinion, what would you choose to do?" What have you written? Are there any surprises? Didn't you always know in your heart that you wanted to:

- Go back to school and earn a degree?
- Skydive?
- Splash paint on a huge canvas?
- Design and build furniture?
- Understand computers?
- Write a novel?
- Walk across the United States?
- Run an English tea shop?
- Give marvelous parties?
- Examine desert flowers?

- Tell fortunes?

- Climb mountains?

- Speak Chinese?

- Play the bassoon?

- Spend a year in Italy?

At first glance, some of your answers will seem wild and totally out of the question. Why? Everything on the list above is attainable—for the person who wants it enough to begin planning. At least *some* of the items on your list can be realized. Indulge yourself! Think only of what you want right now and what would please you *most*. Put aside your feelings of guilt. Forget what people would say. Stop thinking of how the money you would spend, whether much or little, could be used for some more "worthy" purpose. Sift the possible from the unlikely, and begin to think of yourself not as who you *are*, complete and shaped by the life you have led, but as a "work in progress."

Regardless of your age, assuming reasonably good health, it is not too late to change direction. Like launching yourself back into "dating," you'll need courage to discover yourself—to *fall in love with yourself*—to value yourself enough to do what you really want. You'll need to prepare and plan. This may be the most challenging and the most rewarding effort you will ever make.

Albert's Story

"Albert," a fellow student during my undergraduate years, had just turned eighty-two when we marched together to receive our bachelor's degrees. We were all proud that day, but none stood up more straight or smiled more broadly when presented with his diploma than this ever-young elderly man. As a young person, he'd had to help support his brothers and sisters. Later, he was responsible for his own family of sons and daughters. Always bright and inquisitive, he read as much as he could, bringing home bags of books from the library; he couldn't afford to own many books of his own.

His interests were wide: literature, history, archaeology, anthropology. There was hardly a subject he hadn't read about. Even after his children had left home, his responsibilities continued to weigh heavily on him. Abigail, his wife of many years, became disabled. Added to his hours at the plant were the everyday household chores, plus the care of his wife.

Only after he retired from his job on a modest pension did Albert allow his old dream of attaining a college degree to become a possibility. He talked about it, hesitantly at first, with Abigail. She encouraged him to explore his local college. Then Abigail's health declined so sharply that she needed constant care. Albert put his dream aside once more, nursing his wife for several years before she died.

When I first met Albert, he had completed the first two years of college work and was highly respected on the campus. He eagerly participated in the classroom but was wise enough not to take over class discussions, even though he had far more worldly experience and had read more than most of the other students.

Albert loved being a college student. He was on campus every day. He was either studying in the library; experimenting in the chemistry lab; meeting with faculty members; or eating his packed lunch in the quad. He usually ate with a group of young people who might have been his grandchildren or even his great-grandchildren, but were, in this setting, his contemporaries.

At the commencement ceremony, the president of the college presented Albert with a special silk stole to wear over his graduation gown. The entire assembly stood and applauded—and whistled and hollered and shrieked!

Albert did not need a college degree to progress in the world of work. His need was to fulfill himself. He was exceptional in realizing his dream so late in life, but he was not the only mature student on campus even at that time. Now, more and more people are returning to college in their fifties, sixties, and later to earn degrees and, yes, to start new careers—often the kinds of careers that once would have been considered an "indulgence" or simply impossible. Newspapers and magazines like *AARP The Magazine* often run stories about these enterprising men and women.

In the past, few women could aspire to law degrees, but since age is no barrier to practicing law, more and more older people are graduating from law school, hanging out their shingles, and taking cases that interest them. Others become social workers or counselors, often specializing in the concerns of older people. With an aging population, this is a growing field. Still others are able to build small businesses simply by doing what they most enjoy.

Madge's Story

"Madge" had stayed in an unhappy marriage for thirty years, until her last child was launched and independent. She then sued for divorce.

Madge surprised her friends and family by beginning work at an animal shelter, at first earning little more than minimum wage. As she learned more about the laws and ordinances that apply to animals, as she became more knowledgeable about the feeding and breeding of animals, she became more valuable to her employers. Finally, Madge established her own business.

Madge doesn't make a fortune, but she is happier than she has ever been in her life. She regularly walks dogs for busy professionals, she is expanding her kennels, and she has recently begun breeding Irish wolfhounds—a breed she has always loved. She is now so knowledgeable about wolfhounds that she is often called to serve as a consultant to groups devoted to that breed.

Once Madge was "freed" of her job as an "ordinary" housewife and mother, she changed her life completely, finding real joy in doing what she wanted to do.

Olivia's Story

"Olivia," married in her late twenties, lived a conventional and contented life. She prepared baked goods for the PTA, went door-to-door with her daughters as they sold Girl Scout cookies, knitted sweaters of her own design for her family, and watched a lot of television as she waited for her girls to come home from their dates. After her daughters married and left the area, she found an office job in her daughters' old school and held it until she reached retirement age. Only weeks into her retirement, her husband died, leaving her financially comfortable but with nothing much to live for.

After months of mourning—and hours on the telephone with her daughters on the other side of the country—she signed up for an art class at the local community college. She knew she had to do something to fill her days, and she'd always had a good eye for line and color.

Her instructor immediately saw that Olivia had a natural "primitive" talent. She was disappointed that he gave her only the most basic guidance, but he told her he was afraid of spoiling her style by shaping her work in any way. He encouraged her to simply express herself on canvas without regard to artistic traditions or trends.

Within two years, Olivia had produced dozens of marvelously vibrant paintings, some huge, some as tiny as postcards. When I met her, a studio addition to her house, with enormous windows that captured the northern light, was just being completed and she was negotiating with a major gallery for a showing of several paintings. She told me she felt more fulfilled, more truly happy, than at any time in her life.

"I had no idea that I could be, that I was, a real artist. People always enjoyed the little pictures I drew on letters and on birthday cards—but to discover that I can create something seriously beautiful is a real joy."

Your Story?

What about you? You know you have at least one novel simmering in your brain. You've always had a hankering to get it on paper. Why aren't you writing it? Is it too late? Are you too old? Nonsense! Know that the highly acclaimed *Jules and Jim* was written as a first novel by a man in his seventies. Will it take too long? Will you never get it finished? If you type one page a day on your computer or typewriter, you may be able to complete the novel in less than a year. And if you don't turn out those pages, what will you have at the end of that time? Only your unfulfilled longing.

So, you aren't sure how to start? Most bookstores and libraries have shelves of books on planning and structuring a novel. Classes in creative writing abound.

You *can* invent a new identity. You can be a writer or a painter or a mountain climber, or whatever your dream may be. You can be complete and self-sufficient. The love you have been looking for may be hidden within you.

Conclusion

"The Whole World Is Waiting for Me"

*I*f you read Chapter 9, you may remember Sandra's words: "The whole world is waiting for me." Now that you have completed this book, my hope is that you, too, can make this joyous statement.

The world *is* waiting for you! All you need is the courage to go out and meet it. Paul Newman, speaking of what he learned about directing movies, once said that his main task is to find out what gives actors confidence "because it liberates them to do things they wouldn't otherwise do."

My task, too, has been to encourage you to build confidence in yourself, to help you know who you are and what you really want. I have also suggested the many different ways you might look for love and fulfillment, things you wouldn't have otherwise done, but that can yield unimaginable rewards.

PLEASE LET ME HEAR FROM YOU

Almost every day, someone tells me how she met the man in her life, or how a friend or sister or cousin found her husband or companion. I love those stories! They constantly reaffirm that people in later life are looking for and finding affection, romance, and contentment.

Just the other day, my neighbor told me about her friend "Laura," a widow nearing seventy, who recently married a man some nine years younger than she, and who is as happy as any new bride could be. After she was widowed, Laura found that her income would barely cover the upkeep of her house. She hated the thought of moving, so she placed an ad offering a large room and bath for rent. The first renter was a young fellow in his twenties who came and went, but the second man came—and never left. Laura married him.

Here is a case of a knight who actually *did* ride up to the house—although in a Honda Civic, not on a white charger—and carry off his fair lady! It shows that almost anything can happen once you take steps to *make* it happen.

And this morning I heard from an old friend in the Midwest who arranged a "bring a friend" party. Each of the women brought a single man in the right age group, a man with whom she was *not* romantically involved—an office mate or family member, for instance. According to my friend, some fascinating mixing and matching took place!

Love comes in many forms and is found in many places.

The direct resources—personal advertisements, online services, singles events, dances and mixers, dating services, and matchmakers—all are straightforward methods of meeting members of the opposite sex. The indirect resources—a wide range of activities that interest you—are ways of enriching your life and making new friends among men and women who share your passions. Just by being out and involved in the community, you will be in contact with people through whom you may find romance.

Finally, discovering your own creativity and developing your own skills and talents can bring you rewards you never dreamed of. Please let me know *your* story. Which methods work for you? Tell me about your adventures. You can reach me, Monica B. Morris, care of Square One Publishers, 115 Herricks Road, Garden City Park, NY 11040. I'll be waiting for your letters.

Meanwhile, whatever the route you choose, I wish you love.

Useful Resources

A wide range of businesses, online services, books, and other resources can help you in your search for that special someone—or, for that matter, in your search for a new life-enriching activity or interest. Keep in mind that the following list, which is divided by chapters, is intended only to give you a start. Personal recommendations, online searches, and trips to your local library and bookstore are sure to put you in touch with other great resources.

CHAPTER TWO
Picture Yourself

Since a nice photograph of yourself is such an important part of personal ad contacts and computer dating services, you'll want to put your best face forward. Throughout the country, a new generation of fun photo studios specializes in creating that "model" look. Unlike traditional portrait studios, they will provide you with a mini-makeover, including makeup and hairstyle; dress you attractively; and use lighting that makes you both feel and look like a superstar—and they will do it all for a reasonable price.

Glamour Shots is just such an operation, and has franchises across the United States and Canada, many of which are located in shopping malls. For information about the Glamour Shots studio nearest you, log onto www.Glamourshots.com. If none of their franchises is close to you, flip through your local *Yellow Pages* for a similar photo studio. Remember to ask about prices and to view samples of their work before you agree to anything. In this case, a good picture could be worth a thousand dates.

CHAPTER THREE
Online Dating Services

Hundreds of Internet sites offer dating and matchmaking services. New sites are added from time to time, while other sites disappear. Here are some of the more popular current sites.

AmericanSingles.com

This service allows you to create a profile, post photos, and search for members free of charge. A relatively small monthly fee is charged for full access to the site's tools.

Blacksingles.com

Calling itself "the world's largest singles network for people of color," this site provides a variety of services free of charge.

Cmle.com

The Classical Music Lovers' Exchange is a nationwide organization that provides lovers of classical music with access to one another. A monthly membership fee is charged for services.

Concernedsingles.com

The mission of this online service is to bring together socially conscious singles who care about social justice, the environment, racial equality, gender equity, and personal growth. A yearly membership fee is charged for services.

Date.com

Free membership allows you to view the site's profiles and photos, and to send your profile to other members. A membership fee—which can be paid on a monthly or yearly basis—permits access to other services.

DreamMates.com

Boasting over 3 million members, DreamMates offers all services free of charge.

Eharmony.com

Eharmony uses a Personality Profile to create matches between members. The membership fee can be paid on either a monthly or yearly basis.

EightatEight.com

Designed for single professionals, Eight at Eight arranges dinner parties and other social events for four single men and four single women with similar backgrounds and shared interests. The service now covers seven areas—Atlanta, Chicago, Dallas/Fort Worth, Denver, Las Vegas, New York City, and Fort Lauderdale/Palm Beach—and is expanding.

ItsJustLunch.com

It's Just Lunch is a dating service "for busy professionals" that matches singles with similar backgrounds and interests. The emphasis is on laid-back, casual first dates over lunch, brunch, or after-work drinks—rather than dinner. A membership fee is charged for services.

Jdate.com

Billed as "the largest Jewish singles network," Jdate has members in over 200 countries. While certain services are provided free of charge, full services require a membership fee.

Lavalife.com

This site offers three types of encounters—"dating," "relationships," and "intimate encounters." A membership fee is required for full services.

Match.com

This service uses a Total Attraction Matching profile to make compatible matches. A membership fee is required.

Matchmaker.com

This free service allows you to create a profile, post a photo, and receive and respond to e-mails.

Relationship.com

In return for a monthly fee, this site combines an Internet dating service with great tips, tactics, and consultations to help you not just start but also *maintain* a relationship.

Rightstuffdating.com

Geared for "single graduates and faculty of a select group of excellent universities and colleges," The Right Stuff requires not only a membership fee but also proof of graduate or faculty status.

Sciconnect.com
This service is designed for single science professionals and others with an interest in science or nature. Membership fees are relatively low.

Udate.com
Udate creates matches based on a profile that you provide. A variety of fee-based membership plans are available.

YahooPersonals.com
A low membership fee will enable you to connect with other members through e-mail and instant messaging.

CHAPTER FIVE
Volunteer and Membership Organizations

A number of organizations can enrich your life by offering an opportunity to serve others, of by apprising you of opportunities for social involvement. This list should help get you started.

American Association of Retired Persons (AARP)
601 E Street NW
Washington, DC 20049
Phone: (888) 687-2277
Website: www.aarp.org
The nation's largest and most experienced organization of older persons, AARP has more than 2,400 chapters that work for local community welfare, and provide educational and social programs for members, as well as a range of discounts. Membership is available to anyone of age fifty or older.

American Red Cross
2025 E Street NW
Washington, DC 20006
Phone: (202) 303-4498
Website: www.redcross.org
Every year, over one million Americans serve as Red Cross volunteers, organizing youth programs, teaching first aid, helping victims of natural disasters, and providing a range of other important services. Visit the Red Cross website to find your local chapter.

Habitat for Humanity

121 Habitat Street
Americus, GA 31709-3498
Phone: (229) 924-6935, ext. 2551
Website: www.habitat.org
A nonprofit housing organization, Habitat uses volunteer labor to help build simple, affordable housing in partnership with families in need.

Parents Without Partners

1650 South Dixie Highway, Suite 510
Boca Raton, FL 33432
Phone: (561) 391-8833
Website: www.parentswithoutpartners.org
Parents Without Partners provides single parents with an opportunity to enhance personal growth, self-confidence, and sensitivity towards others by offering an environment for support, friendship, and the exchange of parenting techniques. Log onto their website to find a chapter in your area and to learn of local events.

Senior Corps

1201 New York Avenue NW
Washington, DC 20525
Phone: (800) 424-8867
Website: www.seniorcorps.org
Senior Corps was created to tap the skills, talents, and experience of Americans age fifty-five and older. Through RSVP—the Retired and Senior Volunteer Program—seniors can take part in a diverse range of volunteer activities.

The Sierra Club

85 Second Street, 2nd Floor
San Francisco, CA 94105-3441
Phone: (415) 977-5522
Website: www.sierraclub.org
Whether you want to choose from among 340 exciting trips around the world or get involved in environmental politics, membership in the Sierra Club will provide you with all the information you need to get started.

United Way of America
701 North Fairfax Street
Alexandria, VA 22314
Phone: (703) 836-7112
Website: www.unitedway.org
The United Way leads programs, initiatives, and partnerships through-out the United States. Enter your zip code on their website, and find a list of diverse volunteer activities in your area.

VolunteerMatch
Website: www.volunteermatch.org
This website is dedicated to helping you find a great place to volunteer. Just enter your zip code on the home page to find hundreds of volunteer opportunities near you.

Volunteers of America
1660 Duke Street
Alexandria, VA 22314
Phone: (800) 899-0089
Website: www.volunteersofamerica.org
A nonprofit, spiritually based organization, Volunteers of America provides outreach programs that deal with pressing social needs.

Organizations for the Single Traveler

While all adventures are accessible to the single traveler, some organizations and companies offer programs that are particularly well suited to the person traveling alone. Contact these groups, and see what they have to offer.

Adventurous Wench
1515 S. Extension Road, Suite 2015
Mesa, AZ 85210
Phone: (480) 827-3922
Website: www.adventurouswench.com
Geared for the single woman who wants to travel in a group, Adventurous Wench offers active vacations designed with women in mind. Destinations range from the Virgin Islands to Santa Fe to Tuscany, and include not only "soft" adventures such as hiking and rafting, but also spa trips and shopping for those who are interested.

Archaeological Conservancy

Phone: (505) 266-1540

Website: www.archaeologicalconservancy.com

The Conservancy offers conducted archaeological tours ranging in length from four days to two weeks. Tour regions include the American Midwest, Southeast, and Southwest, as well as Mexico and Central and South America.

Crow Canyon Archaeological Center

23390 Road K

Cortez, CO 81321-9908

Phone: (800) 422-8975

Website: www.crowcanyon.org

Crow Canyon's mission is to initiate and conduct archaeological research and public education programs in partnership with American Indians. Adventure travel programs offer people of all ages the chance to learn firsthand about archaeology and culture.

Cruise Ship Centers

1055 West Hastings Street, Suite 400

Vancouver, BC V6E 2E9

Phone: (604) 685-1221

Website: www.cruiseshipcenters.com

This company offers discounted cruise vacations to a range of locations on a variety of cruise lines. Special cruises include trips geared for singles and seniors.

Earthwatch Institute

Website: www.earthwatch.org

Earthwatch engages people worldwide in scientific field research and education to promote the understanding necessary for a sustainable environment.

Elderhostel

11 Avenue de Lafayette

Boston, MA 02111-1746

Phone: (877) 426-8056

Website: www.elderhostel.org

Elderhostel is a not-for-profit organization that provides high-quality, affordable educational adventures for adults of age fifty-five and over.

The Sierra Club
85 Second Street, 2nd Floor
San Francisco, CA 94105
Phone: (415) 977-5500
Website: www.sierraclub.org/outings/
The Sierra Club offers 340 exciting trips to a variety of locations around the world, from Tahoe to Tibet.

Travel Books

The following are available through online bookstores, as well as local bookstores and libraries. Read them for information and inspiration.

Bond, Marybeth. *Gutsy Women: More Travel Tips and Wisdom for the Road.* Travelers' Tales Guides, 2001.

Bond, Marybeth. *A Woman's World: True Stories of Life on the Road.* Travelers' Tales Guides, 2003.

Bond, Marybeth and Pamela Michael. *A Woman's Passion for Travel: More True Stories from a Woman's World.* Travelers' Tales Guides, 1999.

Comer, Catherine and Lavon Swaim. *The Traveling Woman: Great Tips for Safe and Healthy Trips.* Impact Publications, 2001.

Conlon, Faith et al. *A Woman Alone: Travel Tales From Around the Globe.* Seal Press, 2001.

Steinbach, Alice. *Without Reservations: The Travels of an Independent Woman.* Random House Trade Books, 2002.

Swan, Sheila and Peter Laufer. *Safety and Security for Women Who Travel.* Travelers' Tales Guides, 1998.

CHAPTER SIX
Verifying Personal Information

Several books offer both general resources and step-by step instructions for investigating an individual's financial, marital, criminal, and business history.

Blye, Irwin and Ardy Friedberg. *Secrets of a Private Eye: Or How to Be Your Own Private Investigator.* Henry Holt, 1987.

Culligan, Joseph. *When in Doubt, Check Him Out: A Woman's Survival Guide.* Jodere Group, 2001.

King, Dennis. *Get the Facts on Anyone.* Arco Publishing, 1999.

Sankey, Michael and Carl R. Ernst. *Find Public Records Fast: The Complete State, County, and Courthouse Locator.* Facts on Demand Press, 1997.

Sankey, Michael and Peter J. Weber. *Private Records Online.* Facts on Demand Press, 2003.

CHAPTER SEVEN
About Sex: Websites and Videos

Whether you need instruction, stimulation, or inspiration, you are sure to find these websites of interest.

BetterSex
Phone: (800) 955-0888
Website: www.bettersex.com
Visit this website and order *The Couple's Guide to Great Sex Over 40* series by Sinclair Video Library. This series provides good advice and uses nice-looking middle-aged models, rather than the usual eighteen-year-old nubile bodies. The site also offers a range of books, sex toys, and more.

Good Vibrations
Phone: (800) Buyvibe
Website: www.goodvibes.com
Visit this site for adult videos, how-to books, and sex toys.

Xandria Collection
Phone: (800) 242-2823
Website: www.xandria.com
This site offers videos, sex toys, books, and much more.

About Sexually Transmitted Diseases

The following suggested readings on sexually transmitted diseases are available through bookstores, libraries, and online booksellers.

Kolesnikow, Tassia. *Sexually Transmitted Diseases.* Lucent Books, 2003.

Marr, Lisa. *Sexually Transmitted Diseases: A Physician Tells You What You Need to Know.* Johns Hopkins University Press, 1998.

Sacks, Stephen. *The Truth about Herpes.* Gordon Soules Book Publishers, 1997.

Schoeberlein, Deborah. *EveryBody: Preventing HIV and Other Sexually Transmitted Diseases.* RAD Educational Porgrams, 2001.

Index

GUYS GETS GIRL, GIRL GETS GUY

Where to Find Romance and What to Say When You Find It

Larry Glanz and Robert H. Phillips

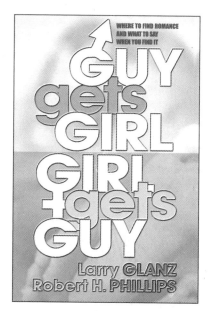

Nobody said that meeting someone is easy. But the fact is that people begin romantic relationships every single day. The trick is to know how to go about it, and this is the book that will let you in on all the secrets and get you started in the right direction. *Guy Gets Girl, Girl Gets Guy* provides all the important basics, including how to successfully meet, greet, and—ultimately—win that special someone.

Guy Gets Girl, Girl Gets Guy takes a practical look at the wheres and how-tos of locating and attracting that one right person. Part One focuses on who you are and who you want to be. It offers proven suggestions for enhancing your "inner" and "outer" assets. It then helps you consider and select the qualities you would like see in your future mate. Once you know who you are and who you would like to meet, the fun begins. Part Two provides a guide to the places you can go to meet new people—from the hottest websites to the trendiest night spots; from new and unusual places to common hangouts that are probably right under your nose.

This book even provides you with clever and effective ice breakers designed to launch your first conversation—a conversation that can lead to that first date, and maybe even a lifetime of love. With *Guy Gets Girl, Girl Gets Guy,* you have no more excuses to be lonely.

About the Authors

Larry Glanz is a relationships expert. He has spent over twenty years studying and analyzing mating customs in the United States. Based on this work, he has developed effective relationship strategies and techniques. He is the coauthor of *How to Start a Romantic Encounter.*

Robert H. Phillips is a practicing psychologist and the director of the Center for Coping located in Westbury, New York. He is the author of eight books and coauthor of the best-selling *Love Tactics.*

$13.95 • 208 pages • 6 x 9-inch quality paperback • Relationships/Love & Romance • ISBN 0-7570-0126-2

OUR SECRET RULES

Why We Do the Things We Do

Jordan Weiss, MD

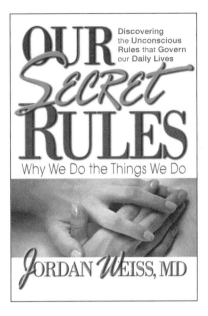

We all live our lives according to a set
of rules that regulate our behaviors.
Some rules are quite clear. These are
conscious beliefs we hold dear. Others,
however, are unconscious. These are
our secret rules, and when we do things
that go against them, we experience
stress, anxiety, apprehension, and
emotional exhaustion—and we never
know why. That is, until now. In *Our
Secret Rules,* Dr. Jordan Weiss offers
a unique system that helps uncover
our most secret rules.

The book begins by explaining the important roles that conscious and
unconscious rules play in our daily existence. Each chapter focuses on a key
area of our lives—money, religion, gender identification, work, friendships,
health, power, personal expression, marriage, and sex. Within each chapter,
there are challenging questions for the reader. The answers provide a
personal look at how we are likely to behave when faced with specific
situations. Each chapter ends with an analysis of potential answers that
is designed to reveal the extent of our secret rules.

Our Secret Rules concludes by explaining how we can use our newly gained
insights to improve the way we feel about ourselves and others. For once
we are aware of our rules, we can then learn to live within their boundaries,
or we can attempt to change them. And as we do, we can enjoy the benefits
of happier, more harmonious lives.

About the Author

Dr. Jordan Weiss received his medical degree from the University of Illinois
Medical School in Chicago. With an emphasis on the body-mind-spirit connection,
he has worked at several leading complementary medical centers. A practicing
psychiatrist for over twenty years, Dr. Weiss currently works at Irvine's Center
for Psychoenergetic Therapy in California. He is the author of several published
articles on emotional responses, and is a highly regarded speaker.

$11.95 • 184 pages • 6 x 9-inch quality paperback • Self-Help/Psychology • ISBN 0-7570-0010-X

12 MAGIC WANDS

The Art of Meeting Life's Challenges

G.G. Bolich, PhD

Magic exists. It is everywhere. It surrounds us and infuses us. It holds the power to transform us. It isn't always easy to see, but then again, it wouldn't be magic if it was. Counselor and educator G.G. Bolich has written *Twelve Magic Wands*—a unique and insightful guide for recognizing the magic in our lives, and then using it to improve our physical, mental, and spiritual selves. It provides a step-by-step program that empowers the reader to meet and conquer life's consistent challenges.

The book begins by explaining what magic is and where it abides. It then offers twelve magic "wands" that can transform one's life for the better. Each wand provides practical tools and exercises to gain control over a specific area, such as friendship and love. Throughout the book, the author presents inspiring true stories of people who have used the magic in their lives to both help themselves and point the way to others.

The world can be a difficult place. Loneliness, disappointments, tragedies, and dead ends can sometimes seem insurmountable. Losing the magic in one's life can make it even more difficult. *Twelve Magic Wands* provides real ways to make it better—first inside, and then out.

About the Author

Dr. G.G. Bolich received his Master's of Divinity from George Fox University in Newberg, Oregon. He earned his first PhD in educational leadership from Gonzaga University in Spokane, Washington, and a second in psychology from The Union Institute in Cincinnati, Ohio. Currently a professor at Webster University in South Carolina, Dr. Bolich has taught courses at the university level since 1975. He also provides private counseling, specializing in trauma resolution, and is the published author of six titles and numerous articles in the fields of psychology, religion, and spirituality. Among his published works are *Psyche's Child, Introduction to Religion,* and *The Christian Scholar.*

$15.95 • 160 pages • 6 x 9-inch quality paperback • Self-Help/Mind, Body, Spirit • ISBN 0-7570-0086-X

Successful Techniques for Getting the One You Love to Love You Back **250,000 COPIES IN PRINT**

LOVE TACTICS

How to Win the One You Want

Thomas W. McKnight and Robert H. Phillips

Maybe that very special someone is not as far out of reach as you think. Maybe what you need are a few effective strategies to finally make the right moves. Even if you're very shy, a little on the quiet side, or simply not the social success you'd like to be, *Love Tactics* may have the answers you've been looking for.

Divided into two sections, *Love Tactics* presents dozens of strategic techniques that are designed to help you in the most exciting search-and-succeed activities of your life. These strategies, which are found in Part One, will help you win the love of that special someone. With each tactic, you'll find yourself becoming more enthusiastic, confident, and eager to approach the person of your dreams in an effort to win his or her love. For those who have already found a romantic partner, but have lost or are in danger of losing that person, Part Two presents tactics for winning back a lost love.

Written in a warm, easy-going style, this book offers a wealth of practical advice on how to get the one you love to love you back. You don't have to settle for anything (or anyone) less. The dream is in sight—and *Love Tactics* is all you need to make that dream a reality.

About the Authors

Thomas W. McKnight is a relationships expert. His columns on meeting the right person have appeared in leading U.S. singles newspapers and magazines over the past fifteen years. He has conducted dozens of relationship workshops throughout the country, and has also appeared on numerous radio and television shows, including Oprah.

Robert H. Phillips is a practicing psychologist and the director of the Center for Coping located in Westbury, New York. He is also the best-selling author of eight books dealing with various chronic health conditions, including *Coping With Lupus* and *Coping With Osteoarthritis*.

$12.95 • 208 pages • 6 x 9-inch paperback • Relationships/Love & Romance • ISBN 0-7570-0037-1